D0776373

Sell Local,
Think Global

Sell Local,
Think Global

50 Innovative Ways to Make a
Chunk of Change and Grow Your Business

By Olga Mizrahi

CAREER
PRESS

Pompton Plains, N.J.

Copyright © 2015 by Olga Mizrahi

All rights reserved under the Pan-American and International Copyright Conventions. This book may not be reproduced, in whole or in part, in any form or by any means electronic or mechanical, including photocopying, recording, or by any information storage and retrieval system now known or hereafter invented, without written permission from the publisher, The Career Press.

SELL LOCAL, THINK GLOBAL
Cover design by Howard Grossman/12E Design
Printed in the U.S.A.

To order this title, please call toll-free 1-800-CAREER-1 (NJ and Canada: 201-848-0310) to order using VISA or MasterCard, or for further information on books from Career Press.

The Career Press, Inc.
220 West Parkway, Unit 12
Pompton Plains, NJ 07444
www.careerpress.com

Library of Congress Cataloging-in-Publication Data
Mizrahi, Olga.
    Sell local, think global : 50 innovative ways to make a chunk of change and grow your business / by Olga Mizrahi.
        pages cm
    Includes index.
    ISBN 978-1-60163-340-8 -- ISBN 978-1-60163-434-4 (ebook)
    1. Small business marketing. 2. Marketing. 3. Internet marketing. 4. Small business--Growth. I. Title.

HF5415.13.M557 2015
658.8--dc23

                                                            2014028056

I dedicate this book to my Googies.

Acknowledgments

My clients, colleges, and collaborators are the inspiration and perspiration behind bringing the wisdom I've earned to print. I sincerely thank Sarah Daniels, Caroline Rath, Judie Vivian, Nathan Tourtellotte, Pat Bramhall, Kimberly Grietzer, Kathleen Deppe, Michelle Patterson, Rose Tafoya, Steve Kinney, Katie Covell, Mark Chapman, Jannelle Salcido, Daniel Tepke, and my number-one proofreader and supporter, Geoffrey Mizrahi.

Special thanks to Rob Hatch, Tony Buzan, Charlene Li, John Lee Dumas, Joy Cropper, Lorenda Phillips, Melissa Jun Rowley, Brenee Brown and Turi Altivilla, for lending your voices to the conversation. Dr. Norah Dunbar graciously gave her social research lens to each chapter, and I am indebted to her. Norah, thank you for crossing over briefly from academia to add to this work.

Jamie Ponchak has been my graphic right hand at ohso! design for the past eight years, and her style has extended to this book. Jamie, I thank you from the bottom of my heart for all the late nights and weekends. Jim Hanson also gets a special acknowledgment for holding down the fort and meeting the demands of our clients with ever-changing technology.

I thank Desiree Lumachi for introducing me to the *Long Beach Post*. It's her special kind of enthusiasm that's been a true catalyst behind my writing. It's also the love and support from The Polish Posse, Bartek Korsak and Monica Petrozolin in particular, that encouraged me to persevere. Thank you for the support of all my family, especially my great Southern California in-laws and my distant, yet close-to-my-heart relatives (Skowronscy!). Avery Mizrahi tops everyone in pure enthusiasm. Thank you for making my heart magically bigger every day, Avery.

A special shout out to Bryan Elliot, without whom I wouldn't have been introduced to some of the great thought leaders who inspire me to write, like Brian Solis, Seth Godin, Chris Brogan, David Merman Scott, and Gary

Vaynerchuk. Contributing to *Behind the Brand* led to many other blogging adventures that allowed me to "ship."

Thank you to the readers and commenters at the *Long Beach Post* and ChunkofChange.com. You inspire me to do my best work.

Thanks to my agent, John Willig and the special author that thought John and I would make a good team, Melissa Giovagnoli Wilson. Finally, a big thank-you and warm West-to-East hug to the fantastic team at Career Press.

Contents

Introduction

Local Is No Longer Strictly Defined by Geography

The things that make us "locals"—independence and uniqueness, the feeling of being part of a community, having Main Street "handshake" integrity, helpfulness, and approachability—continue to remain the same, even as the world around us changes.

Today's global evolution (in the form of new tools, methods, and online resources) can either feel exciting, new, and deliciously ripe with opportunity, or it can create a ball of confusion, pulling you in a million directions.

From Struggle to Success

As a local small business owner, for years I felt the pain of "not enough." Not making enough progress, not having enough money, not growing fast enough, and certainly not having enough time. And, often, "not enough" comes with a bonus pack of the overwhelming feeling of "too much." Too many e-mails, increasing demands, the ever-speeding-up of technology, and a staggering breadth of choices have all caused me paralysis and temporary shutdown.

By all external appearances, I've had it pretty good: an inspiring work space, fulfilling projects, clients that loved what I produced, public accolades, and a house on the water to come home to, complete with a loving family. Therefore, in taking a peek behind the curtain it might be surprising how much of a struggle it was to get the inside me aligned with the outside me.

Case in point: In 2006, I was faced with a crumbling business partnership. My business partner was a graphic genius whose warm heart sold me on a coupling that I felt could never go wrong. When starting our business, we looked at our strengths and came up with a unique value proposition that attracted swift business from large and small companies alike: we married her offline graphics talent with my online e-commerce web design skills. Our "print and online" message was unique for its time, as not many graphic agencies delivered effective web design, and not many web design firms could make attractively designed materials. Alas, after a couple years, the world changed—and we changed—but our offerings and message did not. What she thought we did and what I thought we did diverged. We struggled.

Soon, I spent most of my time connecting the dots on how to most effectively communicate a client's message. I would then look at the channels available to attract commerce strategically—from using the website as a home base, to online marketing, to offline print collateral. At night, I felt burdened with the complex coding that being the "online" end of our partnership required. When I wanted to bring in others to do production, I was met with resistance.

I knew something needed to change. Deep down, I couldn't shake the feeling that I let my partner down—that I failed.

A little bit of soul-searching and a lot of hard work revealed a set of steps, all starting with exploring the fundamental difference in our beliefs in what business we were really in. It forced me to look at what I do best: connect the dots for business by taking oftentimes-complex processes and making results accessible and easy.

As for my partner? I bought her out, started a new chapter by hand-picking a talented team, and moved on. It stung and was liberating at the same time.

As a byproduct, I was introduced to many wonderful people who supported me as my team, resource partners, and advisory board. Opening up to those valuable connections and actually becoming personally vulnerable and raw (paradoxically) led to new strengths.

Choose Me as Your Guide

That painful breakup turned out to be the catalyst that clarified what I do best. It also laid the essential groundwork for the book you are holding now. Today, I serve others by, first, helping them define what they do best and, then, connecting the dots to sales. I light up the path to results by providing easily accessible, low-tech techniques, and I help make sense of the ever-expanding high-tech tools available.

These days, I take on only a select few new clients at ohso! design. I spend the rest of my time connecting with entrepreneurs and business owners through speaking, writing a local business column, serving on advisory boards, and blogging at ChunkofChange.com.

I went from feeling "not enough" to looking at my imperfection as a blessing of human connection. Now, I want to share that feeling with *you*.

Change is happening at a much faster pace than ever—driven by mobile and online expectations that have trickled into the offline world. I'm here to help effectively steer your ship in this sea of change. Even the top marketing chief at Subway recently acknowledged, "There are so many different streams of data and information, and you have to *synthesize them into simple actions* that make sense for your business and your brand." Staying ahead, he said, is all about "testing and learning."[1]

You've made the right choice in letting me be your trusty guide in this series of simple actions; I've personally sweated through each of the 50-plus tips and tricks that follow. As a result of my own learning curve—and invaluable interactions with clients—I've come up with a set of simple steps that allow for essential changes in perspective and process. (Best of all, utilizing this process means that anxiety can't just "take up shop" but, instead, just moves on through.)

With the help of dozens of business owners and hundreds of conversations with experts, I've provided the boiled-down essentials through a series of strategies and tactics. Your job is to find the "Tip" that's going be the real breakthrough for your business.

Just remember: small changes add up. It's as simple as that.

I'm honored and grateful to be trusted with your time, and look forward to connecting with you. Please share with me which Tip ends up clicking with you, and exactly how it makes an impact on your business.

Let's Continue the Conversation

- linkedin.com/in/olgamizrahi
- @olgamizrahi
- fb.com/chunkofchange
- @chunkofchange
- chunkofchange.com

Suggestions for Use

Making the Most Out of Our Time Together

Every jam-packed chapter in this book includes:

- Five Tips that empower you to take action or reflect.

- A "What the Research Says" commentary by Dr. Norah Dunbar.

- An "In the Real World" case study.

- An instructional "Do This, Not That" piece of advice.

Look for helpful callout boxes sprinkled throughout (with information from the boots-on-the-ground experts that guide small business), links to free resources I've developed just for you, and QR codes that direct to great videos.

Note: If your smart phone or tablet doesn't have a QR code scanner built in, I recommend downloading the scan.me app now.

In addition to dozens of local business owners and their stories, featured personalities include:

- Altimeter Group's founder and LinkedIn influencer Charlene Li.
- The man behind Chris Brogan's business operations, Rob Hatch.
- Father of mind mapping, Tony Buzan.

- Entrepreneur on Fire's John Lee Dumas.
- Melissa Jun Rowley, Magic Makers documentarian.
- U of MMA's Turi Altavilla.
- Lorenda Phillips, who has personally coached more than 3,000 entrepreneurs

I'm also excited to share Dr. Norah Dunbar's communications research lens in every chapter. Dr. Dunbar is a professor of communication at the University of California–Santa Barbara whose research has been published in more than 30 journals. Her expertise in nonverbal and interpersonal communication has also been featured in anthologies (such as *The Encyclopedia of Communication Theory*, *The Sage Handbook of Nonverbal Communication*, and *The Sourcebook for Nonverbal Research Measures*). She has been awarded more than $6 million in external grants and contracts from sources such as the National Science Foundation, the Central Intelligence Agency, and the Center for Identification Technology Research.

Get ready to delve into 50 juicy, bite-sized changes that will add up big for you in your business. All of the tips and tricks that follow offer a change in perspective, but most go further to a tangible change in process; all lead you to great results.

Change Your Message

Creating a UVP to Make Marketing Magic

"Why should I choose you?" This anxiety-inducing question is the single focus of this chapter.

Everyone knows that there's a lot of "noise" out there in the marketplace, and in order to overcome the clamor, you really have to stand out. But changing your message isn't simply about altering what you portray to the outside world; it's about pinpointing what it is that makes you different *enough* and then carrying that message around boldly, wherever you go.

All of the tips and tricks that follow are all about determining and disseminating this key differentiation. To get the change that you want and you need for your company, you must undertake the following steps:

1. Understand the points that make you truly unique.

2. Put those succinct ideas down on paper.

3. Make sure that your message is different enough to get through the noise.

4. Be able to communicate your unique value proposition (UVP)—loudly and proudly.

5. Enable the message to worm its way into conversation.

One Step at a Time: What Makes You Unique?

Right now, I'm talking about your message—not the *delivery* method for getting it out there. I'll go into the countless forms of available media, advertising, marketing, and sales opportunities in later chapters. But, talking about delivery channels before the message will do you about as much good as choosing a shipping provider before deciding what exactly you plan to send. No matter what your ultimate medium of choice is or how

> ### Why Choose You?
>
> Successful marketing requires you to identify why your target market should choose you and effectively communicate that to your audience. Focus on two questions:
>
> 1. What makes you different from the crowd (i.e., your UVP)?
>
> 2. Is this different *enough* to provide some sort of irresistible pull to a large enough audience (i.e., your "-est")?

you measure "success," you need to make sure your unique value proposition is crystal clear—then keep stating it, again and again. What exactly is this magic UVP that I keep bringing up?

A **value proposition** is an inherent promise of benefit that a company gives its customers, employees, or business partners. That value is usually measured in terms of "benefit minus cost." A large part of determining value lies in comparing alternatives.

A **unique value proposition** (sometimes called unique selling proposition or USP) communicates the unique contribution your cause, company, products, and/or services are able to provide to the market in a way that is markedly different from your competitors'.

Once you've developed your unique value proposition (see Tip 2 for a free worksheet) and carried it throughout your company, it's time to put it out there in the world, ideally to the right target market that is primed to take it in. In the golden days of advertising, you simply stuck to the essential "four Ps" of marketing: product, place, price, and promotion. In the ensuing decades, as the marketplace changed, that concept evolved: the four Ps became the four Cs (customer needs and wants, convenience, customer cost, and communication), and now there's even an online course that offers the 14 Ps. Unfortunately, all of the acronyms in the world just won't cut it anymore. In a crowded marketplace, what is enough to truly differentiate you from your competition?

Second Verse, Same as the First?

Almost everything that people *need* already exists—and, for the most part, it's all working just fine. So what's the point of bothering to bring anything new to the table, right? Well, even though the vacuum, the fan, and the hand dryer all existed before, Dyson still "reinvented" each one—and made that design innovation the cornerstone of the company's marketing. With that in mind, what is it that's so different about *your* product, service, or cause that it will capture the attention of the right people?

You no longer have a captive audience. You need to truly stand out in order to be noticed. It's not about the "-ers"—"better" or "faster" or "stronger." It's about being markedly different, or what I call the "-est." What are you best at? Friendliest? Most convenient? Cheapest? If you're not stating your unique value proposition clearly and confidently, you get lost in the fray; you'll be ignored. In people's hectic lives, there's no time to ask for clarification. If they don't get your story or want you right now, they will subconsciously press that Google back button in their brain and move on.

The bottom line is, if you can communicate your difference, then there'll be some sort of impression formed in the mind of the customer. If you can't communicate a distinct difference, something worse happens; there's *no* impression formed in the customer's mind. You're ignored; you're an afterthought.

In the next five tips, I'll shine a light on pinpointing your "-est," guiding you in how to write out an effective UVP, then encouraging you to carry it around boldly, to the right people, and get you primed to have them bring your UVP into their conversations with word of mouth.

So, let's get you out there, loud and proud.

Tip 1 Pinpoint Your Unique "-EST"-ness

Differentiate or *die*. It may sound overly dramatic but it is, in fact, that dire. You must be able to get across what makes you different. That is actually the absolute heart and soul of all business strategy. In fact, if you cannot define clearly what makes you different, then there's no point in reading any further.

If you, indeed, have something that makes you different, it's not that complicated to define what that is. There are a host of tools and techniques to help you get to the heart of the matter. I prefer to use "mind mapping" as a group brainstorming technique, but there are plenty of other ways to determine what it is, exactly, that makes your company unique. (For more information on "mind mapping," see Tip 12 in Chapter 3.)

Basically, you need to brainstorm and ask yourself, "Who are we as a company?" It's a big feat to be able to *clearly* and *concisely* answer the question. There are several ways to look at it, though. You can provide several kinds of definitions, including:

- A technical definition, which outlines the specific services or products you're able to provide.

- A character definition that says something about the personality of your group of people.

- A market map definition, which identifies where you fall within your group of competitors.

Again, contrary to popular belief, it's not about the "-ers": bett*er*, fast*er*, cheap*er*. Rather, it's the "-est," something big that needs to be memorable and specific. Take Wal-Mart: the giant retailer isn't just cheaper—it's cheaper on absolutely *everything*. That makes it the cheap-*est*.

What's Your –Est?

Defining that special something that you are especially good at, the core quality that really captures *why* someone should choose you, depends on what you do exactly. Do you sell a product? Provide a service? Champion a cause? Here are a handful of ideas to help hone in on how you can zero in on an effective "–est." Take special note of which items in the following lists resonate with you.

Product Power

You can distinguish your power through:
- High perceived value (i.e., the buyer is pleasantly surprised by the price of your product).
- Unique packaging.
- Standout design.
- Ease of use.
- Unique solution.
- Superior performance over competing products.

For instance, although there are countless donut shops in Portland, Oregon, a new donut maker may still be able to eke out a living. He is significantly more likely to succeed, though, if he can carve out a clear difference. Perhaps he has the cleanest shop in town or offers a special kind of donut that the others don't. In the city that begs you to "keep it weird," maybe it's time to be the most out there! The bottom line is that having a truly unique value proposition determines whether you'll simply exist or find a way to thrive.

UVP and –Est in Action

A few years back, the food truck craze seemed to hit overnight. But what really played out was the perfect dramatization of the importance of understanding your unique value proposition in order to survive.

At first, there were a couple of wildly successful trucks roaming about, updating their ravenous fans about their whereabouts via Twitter. These trucks had very specific, often-never-before-seen fusion menus that had fans following them around town daily. The proprietors of these trucks had nailed down their UVP and carried it out in force, making sure every offering on their limited menus was infused with their signature style.

Before you knew it, though, there seemed to be hordes of food trucks all over. Demand was still high—but so was supply. It wasn't enough to simply have unusual sounding cuisine—every other truck offered fusion features.

At that point, survival depended on having a truly unique proposition that made the truck stand out from a very large crowd, often full of somewhat similar offerings. Yet, on the other hand, that UVP had to not be drawn so narrowly as to appeal only to a very small demographic.

Case in Point: The Grilled Cheese Truck

The original Grilled Cheese Truck (GCT) has undoubtedly proved one of the most successful stars to come out of the food truck craze.

With appearances on the Cooking Channel's *Unique Eats* and Food Network's *Unwrapped* among many, many other TV shows, the GCT has even become a tourist destination for L.A. visitors! After a wildly successful 2009 launch, the enterprise has expanded considerably, with five trucks operating throughout Southern California, three in Phoenix, and two in Austin/San Antonio.[1]

Chef/owner Dave Danhi launched the first truck after entering his now-signature Cheesy Mac and Rib Melt in the 2009 Grilled Cheese Invitational, and seeing just how many hardcore grilled cheese fans existed. His timing was spot-on—the food truck scene was ascendant—and the GCT proved very popular right out of the gate.[2]

By 2011, however, the food truck market had become saturated and—to many critics—"watered down."[3] Instead of good food and solid business planning, every Tom, Dick, and Harry seemed to think of a food truck as easy money, clogging the marketplace and creating an unsustainable industry bubble.

This is where early timing and strength of message came into play for the GCT. Jumping into a growing scene early gave a high-demand/low supply advantage, but *more impor-*  *tantly* for long-term success, the breathing room to establish a strong brand identity with consumers. Key aspects of the GCT formula included excellent food, local food sourcing, and social interaction with customers.

But the GCT did survive—and, as the continuing expansion shows, thrive. Now, it seems that the biggest challenge facing the GCT team comes from dealing with the flip side of brand awareness. Customers new and returning have high expectations about both the food *and* the experience. To truly take the enterprise to the next level through national expansion, they will have to deliver consistently excellent food and customer service to keep the positive buzz alive—and customers coming back for more.

At Your Service: How to Distinguish Your Services

Services, of course, are a bit less defined in their offerings. Yet there are just as many distinguishing features to tell your customers about:

- Faster response time.
- Ability to offer more value for less money.
- High level of expertise.
- Excellent industry reputation.
- Perception that you bring more to the table (intangibles).
- Availability of the service at a particular time of need.

Consider H&R Block. Ever since I can remember, I have associated this company with tax preparation, having accompanied my parents to a brick-and-mortar location on more than one occasion. For a very long time, they held a huge market segment because they provided many of the attributes on the preceding list. Specifically, they provided quick service in advance of tax day each year.

That position took a big hit with the introduction of TurboTax software and then TurboTax online. Instead of schlepping to the nearest H&R Block, anyone could do their own taxes from the comfort of their own home, often for free or a very low fee.

Although TurboTax prices have gone up, they now offer a wealth of informational resources and audit protection guarantees. But newer online tax services have differentiated themselves by touting their "truly free" tax returns and lower prices. H&R Block has also launched a recent marketing counteroffensive by running ads proclaiming that Americans that did their own taxes lost out on more than $1 billion in potential tax refunds last year. In that way, H&R Block emphasized its high level of expertise and ability to help people save or get more money.

Distinguish Your Cause With "–Est"

Even if you're not selling a product or service (as is the case with many nonprofit organizations), you still have to tell people what unique value they'll get for their money, which may include:

- Eliciting emotion by demonstration a "fit" with a particular value system.
- Striking a chord through personal identification with an issue.
- Quelling negative feelings by alleviating an anxiety.
- Providing a tangible incentive, such as a gift with donation.

See this chapter's Standup for the Cure case study as an example of a cause's UVP in action.

So, by now you might have a bunch of adjectives, descriptors, mission statement fluff, and a mishmash of ideas—but, likely, no big, impressive, specific point of difference. That's not only okay, it's encouraged. The identification process is a messy one. Only after you've done some brilliant brainstorming can you distill down your ideas.

Make no mistake: you can still be in business without outlining a clear difference. If you want to be competitive and successful, however, and pull in *more* business (or attract a better *type* of customer) than you would without a clear point of differentiation, you need to figure out what makes you stand apart.

Now, it's time to pare it all down to something that will make a potential customer stop in his or her tracks. In the next tip, I'll guide you in taking your –est to writing out your UVP.

Tip 2 Write Out Your Unique Value Proposition

There are countless books out there that will assist you in writing a mission statement. This is not one of them. A mission statement can be a valuable tool *within* the organization, but does little to establish your company in the minds of consumers.

Rather than examining your mission statement, I urge you to take a look instead at your unique value proposition (UVP). Contrary to popular belief, the two are not synonymous. Your UVP may be *in line* with your mission statement, but they are not one in the same.

Perhaps it would help to explain the differences between the two.

Mission Statement	Unique Value Proposition
• A statement that outlines what your values are and why you are in business.	• A statement that outlines why you belong out there in the competitive marketplace.
• A rallying cry to get everyone within your organization on the same page.	• A singular directive to convey to everyone outside of your organization.
• A familiar message that might be duplicated among different companies.	• A different message that is unique to your company and your company alone.
• An explanation of who you are and what benefits you have to offer.	• An explanation about why you truly stand apart from other companies.
• A wordy and long description.	• A pithy and short description.
• An idea based on internal perceptions.	• An idea based on external perceptions.
• A message for company-wide cohesiveness and investor relations.	• A message for marketplace-wide differentiation and marketing.

It's not just about being valuable; it's about being *unique*. A UVP "sells" a product or service because it differentiates it from other products or services that are available:

- What do you bring to the table that others do not (or cannot)?
- How does someone know that you're good at what you do?
- Where do you specialize?

At this point, it may be helpful to reiterate our definitions: A **value proposition** is an inherent promise of benefit that a company gives its customers, employees, or business partners. That value is usually measured in terms of "benefit minus cost." A large part of determining value lies in comparing alternatives. A **unique value proposition** (sometimes called Unique Selling Proposition or USP) communicates the unique contribution your cause, company, products, and/or services are able to provide to the market in a way that is markedly different from your competitors.

You really do have to understand your competition and be able to recognize where you stand in the marketplace. You can't come up with a UVP unless you understand that you're competing!

A company dealing with a smaller market may not have to dig as deep. It may simply need to clearly communicate what it is that it does. For instance, if you're the only shoe repair service in town, your point of differentiation may be as simple as stating that you *are,* indeed, a shoe repairer.

If there are 15 shoe repair shops, however, you need to be the one that stands out in some way. Perhaps you've been in business the longest, or you're the least expensive, or you're the most experienced with certain types of shoes. In more complex or saturated markets, a company has to answer less about the "how" and more about "how *uniquely.*"

When a marketplace is extremely crowded and competitive (as is the case for realtors and insurance agents), the UVP often boils down to relationship—it's about the personalization (or personalities) in the business. In other words, as a realtor, you might be the "go to" person for a particular street, city, or zip code, or you might just be the friendly, likeable agent that people prefer to do business with.

Keep in mind that your UVP doesn't have to appeal to *everyone*—but, rather, it must resonate with your target market. You are truly homing in on a small percentage of the population. If you're appealing to them well, then you're going to be remembered. Unfortunately, there will always be a portion of the population that ignores you because they just don't need what your company has to offer right now—and that's okay.

Still stumped? It may be easier to look at your UVP from an outsider's perspective. What are other people's perceptions of your business and how it differs from other businesses? You're looking for a statement that is powerful enough so that someone describes you in that very same way that you do. In other words, when someone passes along your business card, what do they say to go along with it?

Go ahead and ask a trusted business partner what he or she says about you to others when referring business to you. Naturally, this exercise has to do with what people say when they're *not* with you. In that regard, it's different from asking for a testimonial, but it's in the same vein.

Where there's a UVP, there's a point of differentiation, communicated clearly, in a way that someone can personally identify with. Once you've identified your UVP, everyone in your organization needs to know what it is *and understand it*—so that they can communicate it to everyone they come in contact with. A great UVP is the complete answer to the "Why choose you?" question.

> **Do This!**
> **(Really, I Mean It, Right Now!)**
>
> It's an easy worksheet I made just for you. Download the newest version of the UVP worksheet at: ChunkofChange.com/bookgoodies.
>
> Want to share it with me? Take a picture with this book (on Facebook or Instagram) and tag me in it. For a limited time, in return, I'll give you a special code that allows you to get a free 20 minute phone consult via clarity.fm directly with me! Looking forward to seeing your UVP!

Tip 3 Carry Your Message Throughout Your Business

It's not enough to know what makes you unique; everyone who works for your company must eat, sleep, and breathe this difference, too. You need to make sure that your specific story is told by all of the various pieces of your business—most importantly, those people that make up your public "face." (And with social media, everyone involved has some degree of forward facing!)

Of course, you can't be all things to all people. Be honest about what it is that you want and what you have to offer. Then, communicate the same, singular unique value proposition across all your materials. If you have a clear unique value proposition, then it will be easy and natural to communicate to your staff.

Think of your favorite retailer, with multiple locations. What are the ways in which that company's message (or unique value proposition) is communicated? How does that company help its employees communicate that message? Do they use particular signage? Do they employ company-specific language (e.g., Starbucks' "grande") and naming conventions (e.g., Disney's "cast members") to engender loyalty?

Now, think of a retailer that fails to convey a consistent message. It may do a poor job of communicating its unique value proposition to its employees, but more likely, the problem is that the company doesn't have a unified message to begin with. If that's the case, then naturally there won't be any consistency in its materials.

There are a host of ways to communicate your unique value proposition to your employees, including internal print materials, intranet sites, office displays, events, and incentives. Of course, for these tactics to really work, you have to cut through the cynicism that today's employees have.

The first step is communicating to employees that you have, in fact, identified your unique value proposition. "Hey, everybody, we *know* that we're better than our competitors because we are...." Then, ask your employees if what you've identified is in line with what they see on the front end.

The fact is that if you can clearly communicate what your UVP is and why you're doing something, it's not difficult to get buy-in. Everybody likes to be number one. Frankly, it doesn't even matter what you're "the best" at, as long as you're "the best" at *something*.

People are proud of where they work when they can clearly understand the benefit and the difference of the product or service they're representing. What is it about your unique value proposition that can make your employees feel like winners? Once you've identified that, your employees will gladly communicate your unique difference to the outside world, with pride.

Tip 4 Get to Know Your Target Audience, Intimately

Picture yourself single and writing an online dating profile. I'm sure you'd be thinking about what people you want to attract, and probably be looking through their profiles first. You may even take the extra credit option of seeing your competition's profiles.

Who Are You Attracting With That Sexy UVP?

Target marketing has to do with breaking your potential global audience into segments, specifically only the potential *buyers* of our product, service, or cause. As much as we might be tempted, we can't be all things to all people. We have to commit and put some stakes in the ground. Are you ready to write your personal ad? Who are you looking for?

Start by thinking about your current and potential customers' wants and needs.

Product development pro Dan Tepke, author of *Hatching the Million Dollar Idea*, explains it beautifully:

Customer need	Consumer wants	Consumer demands
Something essential to life, such as food, water, shelter, clothing, safety, and esteem, to mention a few. These needs can be defined best as essential elements for human survival. If your product is a high-end sports car or a designer wardrobe, these would not be considered needs, but desires.	Desires for specific items that satisfy deeper needs. A want is something someone would **like** to have, even if it is not beneficial. It could even be bad to have. These may include items like Apple's newest It product, a high-end vacation, or a Porsche 911.	Involve not only whether or not our idea is something people want, but also how much and how often they might want it. A customer must have both the willingness and the ability to purchase your product or service on a regular basis.

According to the Small Business Administration, there are two methods used to segment a market:

- **Geographical segmentation.** Specializing in serving the needs of customers in a particular geographical area.
- **Customer segmentation.** Identifying those people most likely to buy the product or service and targeting those groups. [4]

You are selling local, so geo-segmentation should be the easy part. A list of zip codes or neighborhoods you wish to service will suffice. If you are an online business or can service national or global customers in the form of e-commerce, it's important to expand that geo-segmentation to a psycho-demographic model. That way, you'll understand where to focus your efforts in new geographic markets that share the same type of customer. Research has shown that when people move, they move to a similar neighborhood, with a similar makeup of people and services to where they came from.

Some of the most basic questions you should ask in forming an idea of customer segmentation have to do with what these people want, need, think, and feel. No time is wasted from this exercise because it will ultimately lead you to **where** and **with whom** they hang out (their tribe).

Big companies pay for tools like Claritas (owned by Nielson) to explain to them where to find their perfect segment in order to communicate to them. They want to know where all those "02s" live and what media they consume. Curious? Check out your zip code and see if you identify with the psycho-demographic segment of buyers and their definitions by scanning the QR code or Googling "claritas prizm zip code."

Why is that our desired end point? Because that virtual or real (coffee shop, tradeshow, website, search engine, Twitter feed, health fair, street location, event, traditional media), is where I should be hanging out with my product, service, or cause, and shouting my UVP from the rooftops! Taking this thought experiment all the way through will also assist you in the critical understanding of whether the segment is large enough for you to be successful.

Is Your Market Large Enough? Who's In or Out?

Make sure your segment contributing to your bottom line is larger than your biggest fan (mom). Note: your curmudgeonly grandpa that won't buy anything new is not in a segment!

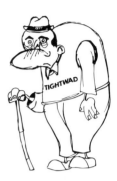

I like using the Personas app to put forth a visual representation of my potential target markets. (See this chapter's "Do This, Not That!" section.) Do not feel limited in putting them in a category up front; once you have enough information, the patterns/psycho-demographic segments should start to emerge more clearly.

What the Research Says With Dr. Norah Dunbar

This chapter is all about identifying your uniqueness (or your "-est") and how to communicate that to the public. It's what social scientists like me call persuasion, social influence, or compliance gaining. There are a few things about persuasion that you should remember:

1. Most persuasion happens outside of our conscious awareness. We are not only persuaded by overt messages (such as advertising), but also by subtle messages (such as the friendliness of your staff, how busy you appear to be, the cleanliness and the décor of your business, the design of your logo, how professional your website looks, how reasonable your prices are, and even whether or not you seem trustworthy). You need to think about the total impression your customers get from your business—not just the messages you're consciously intending to send.

2. Persuasion can happen both on a mass scale and also one-on-one. You could make a YouTube video that goes viral and, in turn, influence millions, or you could treat an individual customer well and have a loyal fan for life. Both are valuable and you should be thinking about both the micro and macro levels of your efforts.

3. There is no one-size-fits-all solution for business problems. Social scientific findings can tell us what general trends are or what persuasion tactics work in most situations, but you know your business or product best. Even when scientists study particular examples in case studies, those cases might be different than your business in some important ways. We can learn from the successes and failures of others but we should still try to customize our messages to our own contexts.

Tip 5 Build Word of Mouth Into Your Product or Service

When we think about the "message" of a business, we usually associate that with how the business communicates with its customers through its marketing efforts. Yet, don't forget that the number one vehicle for your message is the actual product or service you provide. And if you successfully capture your message within your product, then you'll have a very happy customer. But maybe only that one.

So why not take it one step further—and consider how to also build word of mouth into that product? Then, instead of one happy customer reveling solo, you can exponentially multiply that satisfied sentiment.

Let's Give 'Em Something to Talk About

What triggers the urge to spread the word? Several strategies can help infuse your offerings with the type of buzz that gets girlfriends gossiping and social networks zinging:

- Catering to your brand ambassadors (see Tip 22) or other influencers within your target demographic.
- Creating an aura of exclusivity using added perks through loyalty and reward programs.
- Cultivating an "under-the-radar" vibe that paradoxically pushes people into one-up-style revelations.

In 2013, popular restaurant chain Just Salad launched a genius marketing campaign that featured the coveted Pink Bowl, somewhat akin to Wonka's Golden Tickets. Only 100 of these rosy-hued babies got sent out, arriving via mail to demo influencers and loyal customers in an equally pink box, with number 17 landing in the hands of Dave Kerpen, the now chairman of Likeable Media (a self-styled "social media and word of mouth marketing agency")—and a major demographic influencer.

But wait, there's more! The Pink Bowl came imbued with mystical properties that conferred fantastic benefits on its owner. On presentation of the bowl, the owner was entitled to a free salad topping among other perks. But by far the best benefit, the one that got people chattering? The ability to go straight to the front of the line, a big deal given the restaurant's popularity.

Kerpen trumpeted his awesome Pink Bowl experience on a LinkedIn blog post: "I walked past a line of about 40 people, several of which were literally *ooh*-ing and *ah*-ing at my Pink Bowl as I walked. I felt like Moses parting the Red Sea with my Pink Bowl."

Those on queue buzzed excitedly among each other, wondering where he had gotten the mythical bowl, the likes of which the Just Salad counter person had not even seen yet. And a mere glimpse of the pink prize served to quell the complaints of the lady who previously occupied the line's poll position.

Just like that, the story spread like wildfire, starting with the 30-odd Likeable staffers Kerpen told upon his return from his lunch run. A slew of Facebook and Twitter posts launched shortly thereafter. And I'm guessing many of those in line that day, and even the restaurant staff, mentioned it over dinner or cocktails that evening.

Still Stumped?

Maybe you're scratching your head thinking, *"But I sell toilet bowl brushes, which are not especially exciting."* Fear not. Even the most unsexy, utilitarian products can still generate buzz, which means you're only limited by your own lack of imagination.

Prime example: The creative marketing stylings of the folks at Duck Brand duct tape. First, they brought flair to the humble but hard-working adhesive hero by adding hip colors and designs to the previously monochrome colored tape, which upped

its appeal to teenagers across America. Then, the company introduced its annual Stuck at Prom scholarship competition, which challenged teens to craft their prom ensembles completely out of Duck tape.

In addition to encouraging massive sales (the 2013 winning couple alone used 120 rolls), the competition creates big buzz at the high schools of all of the insanely creative participants.

Bring the Buzz

So, start thinking about how to stoke your own buzz. Ask yourself and your team questions like:

- How can we build a community atmosphere where customer-to-customer interaction is part of our business?

- How can we encourage customers to automatically share their experience with their online social groups?

- How can we build teams or teamwork among our customers in ways that support ongoing use of our products or services?

- How can we identify our most loyal customers and channel their already existing enthusiasm into broader customer communication?

- What are some meaningful perks that might add value to our products and/or our customer experience? (Think about no- or low-cost options that are relatively easy to execute versus costly or elaborate rewards plans/systems.)

- How can we reward employees and/or contractors for promoting the business well and taking personal pride/ownership of the brand and its reputation?

Once you begin to look at how to garner attention as a three-dimensional problem, you may be surprised by all of the fresh ideas that spring to mind.

In the Real World: How Understanding UVP Propelled Standup for the Cure's Record-Setting Launch

Identifying your unique value proposition presents different challenges, depending on what exactly you plan to market. I have found that nonprofit organizations find this especially true. That's why I decided to highlight the successful efforts of Standup for the Cure, a nonprofit that's very near and dear to my own heart, to show the power of discovering your UVP.

It may seem strange to discuss marketing strategies in relation to a philanthropic organization. But with 1,409,430 tax-exempt organizations across the U.S.[5]—all fighting for a share of the same charitable giving market—it becomes critical for a nonprofit to identify its UVP and effectively communicate how this distinguishes it from the crowd.

Standup for the Cure

You may or may not know just how passionate the standup paddleboard (SUP) community is about their sport. But breast cancer survivor and avid paddle boarder Judie Vivian did.

Just like Reese's visionary combination of peanut butter and chocolate, Judie thought how great it could be to combine people's love of standup paddleboarding with efforts to raise money for breast cancer research and local health clinics. Thus, Standup for the Cure was born, benefiting the Orange County, California, affiliate of the Susan G. Komen for the Cure.

The nonprofit organization was formed around the idea of fundraising at a standup paddleboard event, where anyone and everyone could have a blast standup paddleboarding in Newport Beach while raising money. With this very different UVP in place, the challenge began to effectively communicate this message and bring in the public support necessary to help the endeavor succeed.

An All-Out Event

Needless to say, the founding members went all out in putting together the first Standup for the Cure event, utilizing every contact and every possible resource to put together a day that every attendee would remember—and want to return to in the future.

A spirit of inclusiveness proved an important aspect to the planning, because the event aimed at reaching beyond members of the standup paddle community. Organizers seized on all the outdoor possibilities offered by the prime Newport Beach venue, making the event highly appealing, whether or not someone wanted to participate in the paddleboard activities.

An Exploration

As fantastic as the planned event was shaping up to be, organizers still felt like something was missing. As an inaugural event in an area with many, many similar-sounding community and philanthropic events, how could they capture public attention and create enough urgency to get people to act by showing up on that particular day? The planned event was definitely different—but would it be different enough?

Essentially, the organizers understood that they needed to translate the Standup for the Cure UVP into an "–est." The initial event, as fabulous as they knew it would be for attendees, was not enough of a pull *by itself*. They still needed an extra something to truly distinguish the organization.

Then the founders hit on an incredible idea, one that would publicize their message, evoke excitement and buzz, and make Standup for the Cure truly stand out: they would call on the SUP community (as well as the public at large) to come together to set a bona fide Guinness Book world record.

World Record Response

Incorporating the world record into the event proved a genius move. It galvanized the community and upped the level of urgency on immediate participation. I mean, how often do you get to set a Guinness world record? This also got the media's attention, giving a unique headline hook that was way more intriguing than just another nonprofit launch event.

The event garnered another est-worthy recognition: SUP The Magazine's Top Philanthropic Effort award.[6] Just one more distinguishing feather in the organization's cap.

Smart Marketing Moves by Standup for the Cure

1. Identifying a very specific UVP of combining a love of standup paddle boarding with a fun way of raising funds for an important cause, "Have Fun and Save Lives."

2. Organizing the best possible event to appeal to both the hardcore standup paddle community, but also the community at large. (You didn't have to know how to SUP to participate.)

3. –Est thinking by boldly incorporating a world record attempt into their first event, which created widespread buzz and an immediate call to attend.

4. Aligning with top brands, including SUP pioneer Rivera Paddleboards, Maui Jim sunglasses, thirst-quenching Kona Brewing Company, gourmet Ruth's Chris Steakhouse, creative agency ohso! design (tooting my own horn there), and Guinness World Records, which lent to the public perception of credibility and legitimacy.

5. Inviting Zane Schweitzer,[7] then an exciting, young up-and-comer and now world-class surf star, to participate and stoke interest within his fan network.

6. Inviting others to initiate their own events and fundraising efforts, creating a network of passionate volunteers/brand ambassadors.

Continued Evolution

The year 2014 marked the third annual Standup for the Cure event in Newport Beach, which brought in more than $125,000, meeting the goal of 1,000 mammograms for women in need.

Now, don't get me wrong. It's not like the world record effort suddenly made everything a piece of cake, marketing-wise. The event still had many other moving parts that all had to come together seamlessly to ensure that participants had an all-around fantastic experience that left them excited about coming back. But coming up with and executing this bold idea definitely helped everything coalesce and drove the level of public support and interest that was needed for the event to be a success.

Interestingly, while everyone seems to remember that a world record was set, no one ever seems to ask what that record was. Just for reference, on May 5, 2012, more than 700 Standup for the Cure participants set the world record for Largest Standup Paddleboard Lesson.

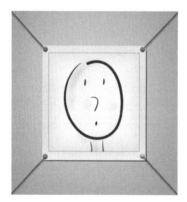

At the end of every chapter is a bite-sized action step that you can take today. At this point, you've already enthusiastically filled out your UVP worksheet mentioned in Tip 2 (available for free in the book goodies at ChunkofChange.com/bookgoodies.) No? Okay, I'll wait....

Welcome back! Now, let's move on to an essential step in changing or clarifying your message—putting a stake in the ground and getting more deeply involved in your potential audience.

Who, what, where, when? Thinking about the attributes of your ideal customer is challenging enough. But keeping them organized inside your already busy brain is likely impossible.

Do: Get detailed about your different customers by utilizing personas, then use tools (like the Personas iOS app for the iPad) that help you map out characteristics of your target customers in visual form.

Don't: Fail to consider the many specific types of customers you serve by adopting the view that *everyone* or *anyone* is your customer.

I often say: "Know your market!" But that does not mean I view it as any small feat. Enter the concept of identifying customer *personas*. A persona is a rendering of a fictional customer—not a fictional *character* whose physical attributes make them real in a readers mind, like in a book. A persona is the embodiment of all of the elements that define the person as a consumer—the things they need, want, and *feel*. What makes that particular type of customer decide to buy?

Some prefer to distill this down to one person as an "avatar," like "Jimmy" for John Lee Dumas of EOfire.com, who I go in detail about in Chapter 10, or a group of people, like the close group of women *Eat, Pray, Love* author Elizabeth Gilbert said she had to keep in mind when writing her latest bestselling book. Imagine the business possibilities if you can think all this through, put it down on paper, and bring this persona to life. And that's precisely the point.

Once you can clearly see your customers, you can understand; you can empathize. You can unlock the mystery of why they buy and how they buy. It allows you to make business decisions with these chief stakeholders in mind. Identifying personas also makes it much easier to know how to communicate with your audience—and, more importantly *where* to communicate with them.

Moreover, the process allows for internal discussion within your business. In developing these personas, you may find that reasonable minds within your organization may differ as to who your customers really are. By collaborating as you develop your personas, you invite valuable debate and insight from your entire crew, while syncing up the company-wide vision of who your team serves.

But why try to organize these disparate qualities in your head? It's like doing long division without using a pencil and paper. Shoot, they even give those brilliant spelling bee kids the chance to write down their answers beforehand.

Instead, use tools (like the Personas iPad app) that give a visual template on which you can superimpose key qualities about how the person thinks and feels, and what they say, do, and see.

Watch each persona come to life—one digital Post-It note at a time—saving each one, and creating a catalog of your most valuable customers.

Change Your Offline Marketing

Bringing Print to Life

Because I've already discussed the basics of UVP and amping up your "-est" in local marketing, in the next two chapters, I will be presenting a few of the tools in your marketing toolbox. First, you'll be looking at some physical marketing tools (*offline*), and then you'll be taking a look at some electronic marketing tools (*online*).

It's important to note that traditional offline products (such as signage and business cards) don't *only* exist in the physical world. On the contrary, you can—and should—use online tools to help with your offline marketing. Sometimes that means simply looking at online examples or following trends on the web. Other times, it means using online vendors (like Moo or Zazzle) for your offline promotions.

It's absolutely shocking to me that there are still professionals (insert air quotes) out there, creating their trifold brochures in Word, using clip art and dated fonts (e.g., Comic Sans or "Disney" font). I cringe when someone hands me a business card with perforated edges that was clearly spit out of their ink jet printer the night before. It's completely unacceptable.

I hate to break it to you, but the printed collateral bar has been raised since 2010, folks. If you *insist* on using a DIY option, a Vistaprint business card is the cheapest option you can still get away with, and if you're already going there, do us all a solid and visit Moo.com's more unique offerings.

The fact is, the Internet has revolutionized the type of offline collateral you can utilize for your business. There are incredible print options out there, in unbelievably low minimum quantities. Just about anything can be custom-made, personalized, and created in odd sizes or shapes.

All you need to do is come up with an eye-catching design (which isn't always as easy as it sounds) and then put it on something people don't expect (which is actually easier than it seems)—whether that's an unusually shaped brochure or a unique piece of swag.

These days, good design and professional printing are expected. It's a *given* that your aesthetic will be impeccable and that your "new" look isn't cliché—whether you're talking about trade show booths or promo items.

Of course, no matter what pretty thing it is that you produce, if you're not communicating your difference (or your "unique value proposition," à la Chapter 1), then you're dead in the water. So, now that I've covered the *why*, let's get right to the *how*.

Tip 6 Update Your Logo

It may seem like a pain to change your letterhead or business cards or signage, but whether you've been around for 15 years or 50, your logo may very well be in need of an update.

Although you may not have thought about it recently, it's altogether possible that your logo is outdated, has become cliché, or uses a font that speaks to an earlier decade.

It's important to recognize that most logos are not "timeless." Just as there are trends in fashion, there are trends in design, as well. Consider it high time to give your image a modern facelift.

Even a brand like Coca-Cola, which has never updated its logo, uses continually fresh design elements and new packaging around a consistent mark. Its competitor, Pepsi, however, redoes its logo every decade or so. (See ChunkofChange.com/bookgoodies for a visual example of the evolution.)

You don't necessarily need to create an entirely new logo, but you may want to freshen it up a bit. An updated logo can energize your employees, excite your existing clients, and capture the attention of brand new customers (see Altimeter Group's subtle logo change in this chapter's In the Real World case study.)

One client, Just Alterations, came to my agency, ohso! design, for a logo-lift. The family-run business came in with a simple lettering mark, hoping for a pictorial logo instead. They wanted some whimsy to accompany their professionalism, and needed to differentiate themselves from local dry cleaners.

{BEFORE}

{AFTER}

JUST ALTERATIONS

Just Alterations chose the needle-and-thread logo option, and proceeded to accent it further by putting an actual straight pin through their business cards. Not only did they use the logo to pump up their cards, they also made the colors and graphics the basis for their store remodeling.

Even so, it wasn't until they participated in the Goldman Sachs 10,000 Small Businesses program that they realized just how far ahead of the competition it put them. Their unique, stand-out logo made others pale in comparison in terms of branding and visual identity, garnering constant compliments and positive feedback.

At this point, you may be asking yourself, "Don't I *already* have a good logo?" Well, if you Google "What makes a good logo?" you'll get more than a million results. Obviously, there's no one right answer to that question.

There are, however, some qualities of logo design that most people tend to agree on:

- Keep it simple.
- Make sure it's legible.
- Strip away all the color to ensure that it still stands up in just black and white.
- Aim for an image that's memorable.
- Note the "feeling" that both the font and image evoke.
- Be unique; try, as best you can, to stand apart from your competitors.

Of course, if these considerations don't give you a whole lot of *specific* direction, that's because it's difficult to put into words something that you react to on an emotional level. Part of the problem is that there's no common language for businesses and their designers to discuss visual aesthetics. There are tools, though, that can help you start a meaningful dialogue.

When starting to re-think your imagery, the first thing you should do is look at a lot of really well-done logos. There's a great series of books called *Logo Lounge* (by Bill Gardner and Catharine Fishel) that are filled with award-winning designs.

These serve as an excellent starting point. Flip through the pages and find logos that speak to you—whether they "work" for your particular business or not—and make a few notes about why they're appealing (i.e., "swirly and feminine" or "aggressive and bold" or "cute and quirky").

Rather than trying to explain what you want your logo to look like—which can be very difficult to put into words—it's easier to give someone a concrete example of what you're attracted to. And, when I say "someone," what I mean is a real live graphic designer.

When you're able to *show* a graphic designer what you like, the process will become a lot easier. "Oh!" the designer will exclaim, upon noticing a pattern you may not have recognized. "He really likes [classic looks, animal icons, edgy designs], etc."

Of course, your logo doesn't necessarily have to utilize a symbol. Sometimes, the right logo is simply a basic shape or a specialized font. (Check out google.com/fonts and MyFonts.com.)

Comic Sans Winery
Modern Wine Makers

Beyond the basic script, illustrative design is a great way to stand out and be unique. That said, if you decide to go with an icon logo, focus on finding the right symbolism. Don't choose an image that doesn't relate to your trade (i.e., a bicycle for a vineyard). Communicate in a clear way what it is that you do.

Ask your graphic designer for three to five distinct options. These should be drastically different, unique images, as opposed to variations on the same design. By having choices that are varied, you'll be able to see clearly what style(s) you're attracted to.

Not only is it okay to have sharp feelings about these looks, it's encouraged. Saying, "I really hate this one because it's too frilly," can actually help your designer. The fact is, your reaction to a logo should be a *visceral* response. You need to have a positive feeling, on a gut level, that the logo you choose represents your business well. At the end of the day, that is more important than a trendy color or up-to-the-minute design.

Of course, make sure to run your logo likes by several people not associated with your business to judge its appropriateness. There may be an, ahem, *unintended* meaning that you don't catch.

Simple or complex, austere or ornate, monochrome or rainbow, there simply isn't one "best" way to design a logo anymore. It used to be a basic tenet of design that a logo needed to look good in newsprint or in a very small format. Often, that ruled out illustrations or detailed pictures. Luckily, the old rules are rarely applicable anymore.

Your logo should shine best on whatever medium it's on the most. If you're online-based, you can use a lot of colors and be more complex; it doesn't much matter how your logo reproduces on paper. If you do a lot of print advertising, however, you're probably going to need to go with something simpler.

Qantas Airlines, for instance, not only took into consideration how their new logo would appear on paper and online, but also how it would look plastered across the tails of all of their aircraft, as well.

Once you've chosen a logo, you'll likely want to make sure you can trademark it. You can (and probably should) hire an attorney if you want to legally trademark your mark. Why is this important? You don't want to be stuck at an unveiling ceremony of your city's new logo, like the recent debacle in the city of Amarillo, Texas, wherein they discovered that their new logo was already trademarked by Emaar Properties.

If legal help is not in the budget at the moment, you can do a quick DIY search (through sites like Trademarkia.com) to see what else is out there—in your business category—before making your final decision.

What the Research Says With Dr. Norah Dunbar

This chapter is all about communicating your brand to your customers offline, especially through the use of your corporate logo.

Dr. James Bowie of Northern Arizona University has been examining the sociological norms behind corporate logos for some time and has studied whether it's better to have a logo that conforms to design norms within an industry or a "deviant" logo that differs from the established norms. His studies reveal some interesting facts about logos:

1. New companies often mimic the logos of existing companies to give themselves legitimacy. For example, Major League Baseball introduced a logo in 1968, with a white silhouette of a player against and red and blue background. When the NBA, the PGA Tour, and a host of other professional sports leagues created logos, many of them modeled the MLB silhouette of a player in red, white, and blue because they wanted to be associated with the "gold standard" of professional sports in America at the time: baseball.

2. Using an unusual logo can be risky if it's too bold a departure from the norm for an industry. The AT&T spinoff company

Lucent Technologies is a famous case study. They chose an unconventional corporate logo compared to those of other technology companies of the tech boom of the 1990s. They chose a simple red circle in a paint-brush style that they called the "Innovation Ring." The logo was scoffed at by industry insiders and employees alike, and was even lampooned in the *Dilbert* comic strip when a logo was created from the stain left by a coffee cup and called "The Brown Ring of Quality." Although the logo was retired when Lucent merged with the larger company Alcatel, in 2006, it remains an example of a deviant logo that might have distracted from Lucent's corporate message.

3. Overall, Bowie found little difference in the longevity of deviant or conforming logos. He used the design categorization system created by the United States Patent and Trademark Office and tracked the "lifespan" of various marks based on their date of trademark filing and date of "death" (due to abandonment, cancellation, or expiration). He found that "deviant" logos had a slightly longer lifespan but the differences in longevity were negligible. There may be too many factors that determine whether a logo (or a company) survives to simply state that deviant logos are better.

Tip 7 Pay Attention to the Most Common Ways You Appear in Print

Every business has print materials that, for the most part, are entirely taken for granted. These pieces of "collateral" are the things you look at every day. And because you use them so often, you probably overlook them completely. It's easy to forget that these items actually help you attract and retain business. Your collateral may include:

- Business Cards.
- Letterhead.
- Envelopes.
- Labels.

- Greeting cards.
- Invitations.
- Postcards.
- Notepads.
- Flyers.
- Brochures.
- Catalogs.
- Sell sheets.
- Product information.
- Visual aids.
- Presentation folders.
- Report covers.
- White papers.
- Newsletters.
- Calendars.
- Hang tags.
- Shelf talkers.
- Rack cards.
- Posters.
- Banners.
- Backlit displays.

Like most, your company's print materials have probably come about piecemeal, out of necessity. It's rare that a business establishes a visual identity and then orders all of its collateral to match. Instead, items are added one at a time, as needed.

As such, it's probably time to step back and bring some awareness to the process by:

- Taking a look at all of your collateral.
- Asking yourself how each piece contributes to your company's "story."
- Making sure there's a point of differentiation between these pieces and your competitors'.

Step 1: Gather

Catalog all of the ways that you appear in print. Then, take photos of each with your smartphone and print out pictures, so that you can see them as a cohesive group. Looking at these things with a fresh pair of eyes, ask yourself the following questions:

- Do these items follow the company's color palette?
- Are all items cohesive in their design?
- Is there a clear visual branding message?

Step 2: Assess

This next step is really about assessing the cohesiveness of your "story." Some might refer to this as a company's "identity," "brand," or "corporate communication," but I like to refer to it as your company's "story."

When you think of the word "story," perhaps you think of a story-book tale. These narratives are: (a) easy to understand, (b) easy to visualize, and (c) easy to re-tell. Your company's story should possess these same qualities.

Perhaps it's a particularly interesting history, the amazingness of a certain product, or the awesomeness of your services. Whatever the story is, it needs to communicate something specific that allows someone to walk away with an understanding of how you're different. It defines your extraordinary point of differentiation.

The fact is that, every time someone sees your printed material, a story is being told—whether you want to tell that story or not. People will make an immediate judgment, based on what you show them. Right away, they'll form a perception of your company and make a subconscious decision about whether they trust you or not.

Thus, if your collateral is not trustworthy—or consistent with your story—potential customers are likely to dismiss you. People do not generally take the time to consciously understand a company's story. If your story isn't communicated clearly, they'll simply move on to the next company that makes sense to them.

For instance, if a company whose story is all about how much they care about the environment did not use recycled paper or soy inks on their letterhead, the result would be rather off-putting.

Ask yourself things like:

- Is my brochure communicating my story in the right way?
- Are my notepads creating a branding message?
- Is my presentation folder drawing attention?
- Is my sell sheet generating enough interest that someone will want to read further?
- Are my report covers presenting my company in a way that is authentic?

Step 3: Differentiate

The third step is about going through a process that makes your pieces stand out from your competitors'.

That may be accomplished by:

- Choice of materials (adding a velvet cover to your restaurant's menu instead of a laminated cover).
- Size (printing thin, tag-like business cards instead of tradition-al-sized cards).
- Shape (handing out a square brochure instead of a tri-fold).
- Feel of the paper (using natural fibers or textured elements instead of plain paper).
- Color (utilizing unusual hues or unexpected palettes instead of the same old colors).
- Design (creating eye-catching visuals instead of a staid corpo-rate logo).
- Photography (employing arresting images instead of stock photography).

If you go through a traditional, local printer (rather than an online printer) you can ask for all sorts of unusual options. Think of all of the choices of greeting cards available out there. There are cards with jewels, tassels, embossing, letter-press, texture, velvet, and so on. In the same vein, as everyday consumers become more demanding in their choices, it's becoming more difficult to stand out just doing a tri-fold brochure.

You've probably come across more than one marketing piece that has captured your attention. Think about why that caught your eye and what advantages it may have over the pieces your company currently has.

Of course, there has to be a balance between creativity and cost. Even if you can't afford a local printer that caters to your every design whim, there are a host of less expensive online choices that will still give you something a little different.

There are countless printable items that you may not have previously thought of as being relevant to your business. For instance, at GreenerPrinter. com, you can create customized stickers, bookmarks, CD sleeves, or door hangers—all in quantities as low as 50.

Ultimately, print cost comes down to quantity. It's often the case that print-

In order to get the creative juices flowing, start looking at all of the sites out there that personalize printed items. Google terms such as: custom printing, eco printing, custom clothing, and more.

Take a look at photo printing sites. Many offer the option to print your photos on all sorts of items in small quantities. In this case, even your headshot could serve as your logo.

ing 1,000 pieces will cost a mere $20 more than printing 500. Of course, if you're not printing 1,000-plus pieces, you'll probably need to go with a digital printer.

If you have the design prowess and creative chops, you can opt for low-cost DIY options like a 3D printer (Afinia.com) or a die-cutting machine that's as simple to use as an ink jet printer (SilhouetteAmerica.com). Low on creativity with these options? Check out Pinterest and YouTube for neat-o ideas.

Good design doesn't have to cost a mint, but it does cost *something*. No matter what the cost of your collateral, it's all about perceived value—the "worth" that high-quality pieces successfully communicate without saying a word.

Tip 8 Create a Press Packet That Will Impress the Media and Key Influencers

Now that you've nailed down your logo and print materials, you'll want to make sure that you're using these things to your advantage by putting your best foot forward with the media and, perhaps more importantly, key influencers.

Creating a great press kit isn't just about making it on to the pages of the *New York Times*; it's about generating a thorough public relations effort. Whether physical or online, press kits are absolutely essential—and they're not *just* for "the press" anymore. The world is hungry for content, in many different forms. If you can get your unique product or service into the hands of a key influencer, it can show up any number of places. Press kits are a great way to reach bloggers (for web reviews) and prominent social media mavens (for promotional posts), as well as traditional journalists (for human interest stories) and editors (for gift guides).

Rest assured if you reach—and impress—an online personality with millions of followers, you can bet that the mainstream media will quickly pick up on your newfound popularity. Business writers, these days, are just as glued to Twitter as they are to the newswire.

To this end, your kit should serve as a one-stop-shop for newcomers to find out about your business and learn why they should be *fascinated* by your brand. To accomplish that, you'll need to do a lot more than just stuff a backgrounder and the CEO's photo in a glossy folder.

Before you hire a writer and designer, start by asking yourself the following questions:

- What *one thing* do you want people who have never heard of your brand to know about it?
- How will you position yourself against your competitors in order to come across as truly *unique* in the marketplace?
- What have you done lately that is interesting enough to be *newsworthy?*
- Once you've pinpointed the ways in which you can stand out, take time to consider your goals. In other words:
- In your opinion, what *one result* would come from a truly successful PR effort?
  - New leads and prospects?
  - More awareness overall?
  - Improved positive sentiment?
  - Increased engagement?

- Inbound links (mentions that lead people to your website)?
- What is your dream "get"? In what news or social outlet would you *most* like to be talked about?

The point of a press kit is to give someone *enough* information—in as easy-to-access a format as humanly possible—so that they can report on your product or service (or use you as an "expert" for a story they're working on). Journalists, editors, and bloggers are busy people with lots and lots of press materials coming across their desks; they want materials that are ready to go. Not only do you have to make an impression, you also have to make your materials easier to access than your competitors'.

Though it's often true that "less is more," your physical press kit should have *all* of the following components. That being said, limit your printouts to a single one-sided page each; someone can always contact you for more information. Finally, keep it lightweight, portable, and smaller than 8.5 ×11 inches. If your kit won't fit in her bag, a journalist won't pick up an oversized kit—no matter how interesting you are.

Although it's tempting to just do an EPK (electronic press kit) and forego the hard copy, I encourage you to invest in a physical kit to hand out, as well. First of all, it creates trust. If you have a well-prepared kit, you're automatically perceived as being that much more "on your game" than the other guys. Second, journalists and bloggers will be more likely to keep you top-of-mind if they have a well-crafted press kit sitting on their desk than if they have to comb through a digital one. Sometimes the old ways are the best ways.

Now, down to brass tacks. Here's a list of what you'll need to insert. Your digital press kit—on your website—should have all of the same components (except for a physical promo item, of course), in an easily downloadable form.

Overview

Include one printed page (one-sided) that presents your company profile. Don't be afraid to spice it up with sexy, newsworthy marketing language. To that end, don't bury the lead! Make sure to put that "one thing" you want people to know right up front. Are you the safest, the least expensive, the most fun? Tell them, right at the top. Get your "-est" from Tip 1 working for you.

Backgrounder

Create a page that offers your company's history. Keep it simple. Journalists will care less about your Great-Grandpa Moses than the fact that you've been in business for 100 years.

Philosophy

This is the place to include your UVP, mission statement, vision statement, and overall company philosophy, albeit succinctly. Don't forget to talk about your "-est." What are you the *best* at? What drives you to do what you do? Where are you headed and *why* are you headed that way?

Fact Sheet

Insert a short, bullet-pointed list of your company's most popular products and their prices. (Even if you're a service-based business, you should include your rates.) Don't bother with a catalog; they will almost always get thrown away.

FAQs

Answer the most commonly asked questions about your products or services. Think like a reporter and try to anticipate the kinds of questions you might be asked.

Staff Biographies

Journalists may want to interview a key executive. Offer super-short bios of your CEO, CMO, CIO, or anyone on the inside with media training. No need to include everyone. Again, keep it to one page.

Brochure

Insert one piece of collateral that you would give to a prospective customer. Make sure it *sells!*

Press Release

Include only *one* press release: your most recent one. Again, make it something newsworthy. Give journalists a reason to write about you. Did you re-vamp your website, release a new product, run a contest, or change your tagline? Let the world know!

Press Clips

Scan copies of any recent press mentions you've received, whether in print or online. If you've appeared in any magazines, insert images of the covers. Whenever one credible source mentions you, others will feel more comfortable following suit.

Reviews and Testimonials

Are people raving about you? Share those accolades! Don't be afraid to edit and shorten. Testimonials shouldn't be longer than two sentences. You can always just include keywords, as well. ("Best ever!" "Life-changing!" "Inspiring!")

Images

If you sell products, it's imperative to have a USB flash drive with high-resolution images available. In addition, you should also include a page with thumbnail image printouts (so editors don't have to actually open the thumb drive). They're significantly more likely to use one of your images for a story if they don't have to go combing through the USB drive to find one they like. Even if you don't sell a product, it's important to have images available for stories: photos of the executives, your building, your logo, etc. You can drive them to a link as well, but the USB serves a useful purpose in that it is available offline, anytime. I'm sure I'm not the only one who has taken some time on a flight from New York to Los Angeles to read through offline print materials and do some focused work on my laptop.

Contact Information

Provide contact information for all of your key executives and press team. Include e-mail addresses, phone numbers with extensions, and Skype screen names. Make it easy for people to reach the right person and, if possible, offer both West Coast and East Coast contacts.

Your Product or a Promotional Item

Enclose or attach a sample of your product or, if you're in a service business, a promotional item that will serve as a visual reminder of your company.

To the last point, editors and bloggers love swag. But they don't love junk. An editor recently told me, in disgust, how sick she was of throwing away logo-embossed mirrors, sticky notes, pens, and calendars that seem to say, "We love to spend money on useless things." On the other hand, she's kept every roll of fashion tape, business card holder, leather-bound notepad, and pair of foldable flats.

The Disabled American Veterans organization gets a response rate of about 18 percent from its postal mail requests for donations. When the mailing is accompanied by an unsolicited gift (such as address labels), however, the success rate jumps to 35 percent. When people receive a gift, there's a subconscious need to return the favor.

Writers will want to try your product to see if it's something worth sharing with their readers, but there's more to it than that. I'll probably get in a lot of hot water for saying so, but people are easily influenced by gifts—and members of the media are no different.

Whatever you decide to include, carry your press kits and products with you everywhere you go: trade shows (both in the press room and at your booth), certainly, but also networking events, client meetings, and coffee dates. You never know when you'll run into a popular nighttime mommy blogger.

Tip 9 Pump Up Your Promotional Items

Sometimes trade shows are a necessary evil. No discussion about trade shows would be complete without a conversation about promotional items. The age-old question, two weeks before the big event, is almost always "What on earth are we going to hand out at the show?"

Is it actually important to have swag? In a word, yes. Studies have shown that promotional items are more memorable than either print or TV advertising. In addition, according to the

Foldable flip-flops from Footprints USA

Incomm Center for Trade Show Research and Sales Training, "Event attendees are 52 percent more likely to stop by your exhibit if you have appealing promotional items to give them." These factors make it easy to see why the promotional products industry is worth an estimated $20 billion. The tricky part when it comes to promotional items is cost. Of course you want to have something original and unique, but you also need to keep your per-item cost down.

First of all, keep in mind that promotional items will not necessarily show a tangible return on investment (ROI). These are not advertisements. Rather, they should be thought of as a PR effort—which makes it difficult to determine a direct ROI. As such, treat promotional items as a marketing expense. You should definitely have a budget for them. Some companies budget this expenditure as a percentage of their trade show costs; others put pieces into their larger annual marketing budget, giving promotional items staying power, beyond the actual event.

Now, what exactly you give to your customers and potential customers is another story. For reference, the top five best-selling items are currently:

1. Wearables.
2. Writing instruments.
3. Bags.
4. Calendars.
5. Drinkware.

Of course, there are countless other options. The hard part is choosing just the right thing. It may seem difficult, at first, to come up with a truly original promotional product. Go for something useful or cute that has at least a loose tie-in to what you do. Start looking for cool swag on the web. Even if you come across items out of your price range, they are likely to spark new ideas.

Check out these sites:

- PPIblog.com (Archives).
- IMC-Miracles.com.
- PromotionalProductInc.com.

These blogs and online vendors offer tons of incredibly creative items, including:

1. Use-at-home personalized branding iron for the barbeque.
2. Logo-embossed Sudoku and crossword puzzle books.
3. Branded "Chairless," the portable seating strap.
4. Printed pet bandanas.
5. Engraved pocket watches.
6. Men's dress socks with embroidered logo.
7. "Foot in the door" branded doorstop.
8. Modeling clay with imprinted lid.
9. Logo-stamped cell phone charging station.
10. Co-branded items (such as a Museum of Modern Art clock or a Swarovski-encrusted USB drive).

These are just a few ideas. In general, there are three schools of thought when it comes to choosing promotional items:

1. Invest in a small quantity of high-end branded items to gift only to special clients and hot leads. In order to have a greater perceived value, these items need to be discreet in their logo placement and should look expensive. (For example: engraved crystal, silver picture frames, leather passport holder.)

    Though this is the least utilized option, for certain compa-nies—specifically, those that have a small target pool of desir-able leads—it offers the most "bang for the buck." If you're giv-ing away something that costs more than $5, ask yourself:

    •   How can we turn this item into a *present* that's perceived as a valuable gift?

    •   Is this piece incredibly unique?

    •   Will this item end up in a prominent place in the office or home of the recipient?

2. Spend less per item and buy more pieces. Hand swag or goodie bags (stuffed with accompanying collateral) out only to peo-ple who actually visit your booth. These useful, cool takeaways reinforce the branding effort and, as such, should be able to be used long-term *or* given away at a later date. (For example: keychains, magnets, or pens.)

This is probably the most popular option. If this is the path you choose, ask yourself:

- Am I doing something different from my competitors?
- Does this item align with my "story"?
- Does this item relate to the majority of my potential customers?

There are so many other options to choose from, but if you *insist* on getting a pen, make sure it's drastically different from everyone else's pen. For instance, during one trade show, Google sponsored a nightclub event at which they gave away LED flashing pens. These could be used as party glow sticks at the event itself and then be kept as fun reminders of the night.

3. Buy mass quantities of very inexpensive items to give to almost everyone in attendance. These short-lifespan items will serve as a branding effort at the show—directing people to your booth or guiding them toward a specific desired action. (For example: custom-wrapped water bottles, branded lanyards, or logo hand fans.)

It's perfectly acceptable to buy inexpensive items! Don't buy something simply because it's 25 cents, though. Ask yourself:

- Does this particular low-cost item actually go with our overall image?
- Does the item serve a specific purpose?
- Is the message on the item intended to result in a specific action?
- Does our logo and company name fit comfortably on the item?
- If it's more than an overall branding effort, is our contact information included?

Whether you choose an expensive gift targeted at a deserving lead or a pennies-on-the-dollar option that papers the convention floor with your company's name (or a combination of the two), the important thing is to recognize that there is a strategy involved to choosing a promotional product. Rather than just opting for the least expensive swag, you'll get a better result when you align your promotions with your prospects. The bottom line is to use your giveaways to stand out from your competition and produce memorable impressions.

Tip 10 Be Open to the Possibility of Alliances

Strategic alliances are probably the most overlooked form of offline marketing and, yet, they're one of the most meaningful. Two heads are better than one and, in many cases, two companies are better than one—especially when they combine resources or share expertise in order to build new business.

Many of us tend to be so individualistic that sometimes it's hard to consider relying on someone else. Don't think of alliances as handing over part of your business, though. Rather, alliances are just like networking. They're almost an extension of the adage "It's not *what* you know, it's *who* you know."

This isn't rocket science. It's simply a way of thinking about your current relationships in a different way, and looking to the outside to form new relationships. Open your eyes to all different kinds of possible alliances, including:

- Key customers.
- Industry leaders.
- Any part of the supply chain.
- Nonprofit organizations.
- Trade associations.
- Chambers of commerce.
- Former employers.
- Recent employees.
- Competitors.

Whether through a formal contract or a gentleman's handshake, alliances can take many different forms. The best alliances are completely voluntary, open-ended relationships that either party can leave at any time. These may come in the form of real-world partnerships or may exist only online. Consider the following methods of collaboration, with varied strategic benefits:

- Advertising together.
- Sharing marketing efforts.
- Sharing trade show booth space.
- Co-authoring presentations.
- Co-branding promotional products.
- Offering referrals (with or without commissions).
- Redirecting business to each other's websites.
- Becoming "certified" by another company.
- Forming "preferred supplier" relationships.
- Integrating with noncompeting parts of the supply chain.
- Franchising.
- Sharing information and advice, as a "brain trust."

According to studies in the United States by Booz, Allen & Hamilton, in the past 25 years, the number of alliances has grown by 25 percent each year. There's good reason for that kind of growth. There are a host of benefits to these types of relationships, including:

- Saving money on shared expenses.
- Expanding your customer base.
- Utilizing a partner's expertise in a given area.
- Having a trusted advisor.
- Capitalizing on another company's size or prestige.

Some of the most popular alliances are demographic or geographic relationships. The key here is to ask, "Is there a company with a product or service that overlaps with my target audience and that I can partner with for a win/win scenario?"

Companies in the wedding business are particularly adept at demographic alliances. (View the video by scanning the QR code on the right.) Jay's, a wedding catering service in Southern California, holds a tasting event once every eight weeks. Not only do they have engaged couples try out all of their dishes, they also have on hand local florists, photographers,

wedding location coordinators, and wedding planners. In this scenario, by acting as a one-stop shop for couples, every vendor wins.

Another good example of a geographic alliance is the local coffee shop that displays an impressive arrangement of fresh flowers on its front counter, provided by a florist located just a few doors down. The coffee shop receives a beautiful addition to their décor, while the florist gets to reach out to potential customers in the area that may not have otherwise been aware of its services.

FEEL LIKE A SUPERHERO

Some alliances are both demographic *and* geographic, but go beyond those factors, as well. Relationships with vendors or suppliers are also key places to cultivate alliances. For instance, Long Beach personal trainer Clint Bigham of We Fit Gym inadvertently formed an alliance with one of his vendors, TurboSonic machines. Because Clint couldn't afford to purchase TurboSonic's entire line of exercise equipment, he asked the manufacturer if he could act as a trial facility for their products. Now, when a Southern California customer calls TurboSonic wanting to try out the equipment, the company sends them to Clint's gym. Clint gets to meet with potential new clients, and TurboSonic gets to show off its products without having to open a showroom. Furthermore, because of their continued use in the gym, some of Clint's current clients have bought TurboSonic machines for their own personal use.

It may seem intimidating at first, but it's not all that difficult to form alliances. (Think of it as networking with a purpose.) First, look for a common customer or audience. Once you've identified a company that fits the bill, open the lines of communication. Then, answer the following questions for your potential partner:

- What can we package together to save money?
- How can we work together to expand our reach?
- What resources can we offer one another?
- How is this a win-win for both parties?

The last question is the most important. There *must* be a win-win situation in order for an alliance to work. There's always "consideration"—a value bargained for by both parties. Nobody gets something for nothing.

In the Real World: Altimeter Group Uses Different Logo Design Strategies to Suit Different Needs

Most, if not all, new business owners view their logo as an important part of their overall identity, whether they plan on using that logo only on their website or plan to incorporate it into a wide range of marketing and branding materials. Some businesses work with solo or small graphic design professionals, whereas others engage major agencies for a multi-tiered campaign.

I e-mailed about the subtle evolution of Altimeter Group's logo with its founding partner, Charlene Li. Altimeter Group's mission, Li says, "is to help leaders make tough decisions by providing research-based advisory on disruptive technologies. We focus on five areas: leadership, digital transformation, content strategy, data disruption, and social business."

Altimeter has undergone two logo designs in recent years, first in 2009, then in early 2014. Interestingly, Li utilized completely different methods to accomplish these redesigns—crowd sourcing in 2009 and then agency design in 2014. Both methods had surprising benefits and also unexpected challenges.

Successfully Crowdsourcing a Logo

The first incarnation of the Altimeter logo was crowd sourced from the marketplace CrowdSpring.com. Crowd sourcing was still a new concept in 2009, but Li felt it was viable given the limited scope of the assignment. "For the scope of my logo needs, I had a clear sense of the brand and didn't need all of the support that a formal branding and logo process required. I just needed a good logo that met the detailed specs I provided with the project," she explained on the Altimeter blog.

To get things started, Li posted to CrowdSpring a brief but detailed description[1] of her background, the new company's mission, and Altimeter's target clientele to give context to the assignment. She also explained why she chose the Altimeter moniker, "It's an instrument used to tell you your altitude. I give a 'reading,' so to speak, on where emerging technologies are heading…. [T]he gauge/instrument aspect is that I provide a consistent, hype-resistant view into the world, objective, reliable, and trustworthy. This last point is important to stress. The logo has to invoke trust and integrity, but also clarity and simplicity."[1] She also gave some general design guidelines, and, importantly, provided specific examples of other logos to help illustrate her preferences.

Li set a two-week submission window, after which time she planned to award $400 for her favorite design. "I was amazed by the quality and quantity of responses," she told me of the 146 designs that poured in. She was also surprised to discover that many submissions came from pro designers; she initially shared the common misconception "that it's students and creatives just starting out that use the crowdsourcing sites."[2] Li took the time to give feedback to each and every submission, "because I was grateful that these designers took the time to submit a concept."

In the end, Li decided to give two $400 awards, because she was torn between two designs—both created by professional designers—and couldn't settle on one by the deadline.

Unexpected Blowback

Although the CrowdSpring group design process had gone smoothly, Li encountered an unforeseen challenge: Criticism from members of the design community who questioned Li's decision to use crowdsourcing, which they viewed as discount services that undercut seasoned professionals.

"As an independent consultant just starting out, I don't have the budget to engage a design agency to do a logo design for me—believe me, I wish I did!" Li said in a blog post. "As such, my logo design options were to work with organizations like LogoWorks, find someone willing to work at my budget through a referral and cross my fingers, or give CrowdSpring a try to tap into the market for new, unknown talent."

"I wanted to provide some background on the two different approaches I took to designing the logo and site, especially as the NO!SPEC community has taken umbrage with my use of CrowdSpring," Li wrote in 2009, in defense of her crowdsourcing foray. "I believe there is a time and place for different approaches to brand marketing and design. In relation to logos, I have done projects that ranged from an agency-led, tens of thousands of dollars logo and branding for a new online product to paying LogoWorks a few hundred dollars for a few designs.... I would definitely use sites like CrowdSpring again. But they do not spell the death of agencies or creative designers, as the iterative, collaborative process is still very much needed and alive."

Large Scale Redesign

Altimeter's latest logo design was part of a much larger brand and marketing overhaul. "Our current logo design was a by-product of an overall brand and website design overview," Li told me. Though the 2009 logo experience had been positive, "It would have been difficult for is to crowd source a complex project such as this one."

So what did Li take from both experiences? "The first thing we did in both was to describe our mission and purpose with stories about how

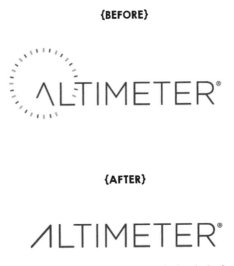

{BEFORE}

{AFTER}

we see the [company/client] relationship. If they can understand the 'why' of what we do, the logo design is then a reflection and articulation of the how."

How does the new logo help communicate Altimeter's unique value proposition? "Our UVP in simple terms is to help our clients—the pilots—soar," Li explained. "Altimeter is a tool and resource to help them do this and the logo reflects the aeronautical lines of an altimeter and also leans into the wind."

In terms of her logo experiences, Li has done just that as well. By knowing the parameters of each project, working with designers to clearly convey what she wanted, and being open to trying new creative forums, she accomplished her logo goals while developing a highly useful knowledge base for best practices.

Do: Buy a logo from BrandCrowd.com.

If you must *buy* a logo, rather than having one custom-created, buy from a company that can guarantee you a unique identifier, like BrandCrowd.com. As a bonus, many of the site's unique logos include a domain name that you have the option of purchasing.

Don't: Don't buy a logo from an overseas logo "factory."

If you're not purchasing an exclusive logo, you might be unpleasantly surprised with the company you keep. There's simply no way of knowing which businesses may share your same visual mark.

The bottom line is that you just *can't* get a good logo for $50. The low end at BrandCrowd is about $250, and a custom design costs $1,500 or more.

Of course, if you have the budget for it, use a designer. Browse the "talent" profiles on CreativeHotlist.com/Browse/Talent, search for keyword "logo," and contact local designers who have portfolios you gravitate toward.

Just remember, as with many things, you get what you pay for!

Change Your Website

Examining the Audience

We've all heard the phrase "You never get a second chance to make a first impression." Nowhere is that more true than *online*. In person, if you don't put your best foot forward, you affect only that one instance, that one encounter. Online, though, you're affecting relationships *en masse*, every time someone new encounters your website. You're basically out there 24/7, "meeting" new people. And most people will check you out online before they check you out in person. It's simply how we, as a society, operate now.

Consider that, currently, one in three couples meet online.[1] Now, venture a guess as to how many people meet *companies* online. When you start thinking about those kinds of numbers, the importance of a great "first impression" is clear. Thus, it may very well be time to update your online visage: your website.

There's a competition between "you never get a second chance to make a first impression" versus "perfect is the enemy of good." You really have to find a balance between the two. Don't let your desire for perfection result in inaction. Instead, revise pieces of your website in small increments—and keep on changing. You may never have a chance at a first impression if no one can find you online, and that's why we are going to look at how attractive you are to search engines in this chapter, too.

People tend to think that once they build a website, they're done. Having a website, though, is a little like having a pet. It's something that has to be continually groomed and cared for. So, think of your website as a constantly evolving entity.

> **Landing Page**
>
> This single web page appears in response to clicking on a search result or an online advertisement. It is likely to feature copy that is directly related to the specific search terms, advertisement, or link. The primary goal of a landing page is to increase conversion (i.e., generate more leads or make additional sales).

Your ideas may change; your technology may change. You may have a seasonal change or a content change. Your decisions today aren't set in stone; they actually have an expiration date. It's an ongoing process and, ideally—even if you're starting from scratch—you'll want to continue to make micro-adjustments over time.

If you can afford to make real-time changes, consider a clean slate. You can temporarily put up a well-designed, well-communicated one-pager. Most of the time, it's better than a complex, multi-layered website that *doesn't work*. Of course, that one-pager must look good and actually communicate something to your audience. Just saying "under construction" or "coming soon" is akin to saying "I'm not ready to do business with you."

You can, in fact, make a good impression with simply a landing page (as long as it's done well). Then, you can make even better "first impressions" with your new webpages, once you release them.

If you don't already have a website, but know you need to get something up, take a moment to write out, on paper, what you want the site to communicate and what results you are expecting from it. Get a designer to express that in one page, with really clean graphics. *Then*, start working on the rest of the site—well, Phase One of the site, anyhow.

If you have a very active site (or an e-commerce site) and can't afford to be offline for so much as a day, consider bringing on a specialist that can analyze your current site and make suggestions to maximize its profitability. For example, search data—or a heat map that analyzes eye tracking—may be used to uncover what users are looking for but can't easily find. The result might be some skillful re-arranging that can increase traffic to your less-traveled pages. Luckily, there is technology out there that can help you test new versions of your website to make sure that you're getting the desired effect *before* you implement site-wide changes.

Peeping Robots

It's likely that no matter what your research reveals, you'll decide to make changes to your site. If you're putting together new stuff that's not quite ready for primetime, however, be sure to include a robots.txt file.

Robots (also called "bots" or "spiders") are programs that search engines use to crawl the many sites and pages on the web. The way to exclude robots from looking at particular files on a server (where your website lives) is to include a robots.txt file.

This simple text file sits in the main directory of your server and is formatted a special way. (Do a Google search for "robots.txt template" to get a clearer picture.)

Keep in mind, however, that the only way you can truly restrict access to information on your server is to create a password-protected directory. If your competition is savvy enough, they may look at your robots.txt file to discover what you don't want the search engines to find.

In the five tips that follow, I'll delineate what success really means, identify your true audience, discuss the importance of gathering assets, learn about the user experience and search engine optimization (SEO), and explain the inner workings of real life website testing.

Tip 11 Identify What "Success" Is

So, you already know that the "when" is 24/7 and the "where" is online. The most overlooked question, however, is the "why." In general, a business doesn't think about *why* it needs to have a website. It just knows that it needs to *have* one.

If you wanted to build a house, you'd probably consult with a few specialists. Just like you would hire an architect to help you visualize a space *before* you'd give a contractor the green light to start building, you need to conceptualize the structure and vision behind your website before actually building it.

Having a distinct vision in mind can help answer *why* you need a website in the first place. In other words, it can help you to identify what makes for a *successful* website. Perhaps it's "We want to bring in more business," or "We want to be recognized for our talents" or "We want to be perceived as a big, important organization." To hone in on that idea of success, you need to answer these questions:

- What do you really want to communicate?
- To whom?
- And how?

Of course, you need to identify what "success" is for your business as a whole, as well. I hope that you've already identified that, but if you haven't thought about it in a while, this might serve as a good impetus to re-examine your idea of success. Your website is part of the "story" of your overall business. Thus, the message you're sending out online should reflect what you're saying offline.

Spend an afternoon researching your competitors' sites and dissect what about their sites works and doesn't work. That should set you off in the right direction. If you really feel like an overachiever, you can create a spreadsheet of the features of each site in order to compare them. (Get a free Google Docs spreadsheet that you can use to track competitors at ChunkofChange.com/bookgoodies.)

Determining what success is will be individual to each type of website. You need to identify whether success for you means simply hearing positive feedback or whether it is tied to a much larger set of analytical goals.

Many companies measure the success of their sites *subjectively*. For example, your CEO or the business owner is happy about the way his bio and headshot look on screen. Those kinds of things are important as anecdotes and, for some, they may very well be the definition of success.

For most businesses, though, it has to come down to something *objective* that can be measured. For example, 100 unique visitors came to your site on Monday and 20 of them purchased your product. You need to be able to determine what you're *getting back* from your site.

What is success for *your* site? Perhaps one (or more) of these reasons resonates with you.

- We have established credibility just by having a website.
- Our brand is being viewed more favorably by visitors.
- We are getting more qualified leads.
- We are able to increase internal efficiency by having forms available online.
- Visitors are viewing our video, which leads them to download our app.
- Visitors are reading more of our blog articles.
- We are increasing engagement and seeing more comments and reviews.
- We are selling more items online.
- We are increasing revenue per visitor (RPV) over time.

The ultimate objective measure is whether your website contributes positively to your bottom line. How you arrive at that measurement is the fodder for measurement and analysis (which I'll delve into in Chapter 4).

Tip 12 Figure Out Who Your Audience Really Is

When most companies think about their website's visitors, they think only of potential customers. Just as there are varying ideas of success, however, there are a host of other audiences to consider, as well.

The web is the only medium where you can create one-to-one relationships by the thousands. That said, you really don't know much about the people who are "meeting" you. Identifying the audience isn't just about pinpointing the demographics of your visitors. It is also about looking at the different categories of individuals coming to your site with varied purposes.

Most business owners want to put forth a sales message, but they're not seeing the full picture. You need to have a message for all of the different people visiting your site, whether they're buying or not.

So, how do you figure out who's visiting your site?

I use the technique of "mind mapping" with my clients, but you can use any type of brainstorming that suits you. Essentially, you want to engage in any kind of free-flowing exercise, wherein one idea can grow organically from another. It's all about generating new and unexpected ideas.

Basically, you need to get away from a linear way of thinking and get into more of an artistic mode. It's not about being pretty, though. Actually, mind maps are pretty messy. That's part of the process.

Get a small group of stakeholders in one room in front of a big, old whiteboard. (There should be more than two people, but probably less than 10, or it becomes impossible to write out what everyone's saying.) Whatever comes out of it, take a picture. Then, have attendees e-mail the organizer with the top thing they took away from the session. This exercise is not meant to be overwhelming or be "all things to all people," but it can help you prioritize your message.

From the Mouth of Tony Buzan, the "Father" of Mind Mapping

Learning how to learn is one of life's most important skills. There are many reasons why mind maps are often referred to as "the ultimate thinking tool," and that is simply because they mirror the way your brain functions.

Being able to reflect the *radiant* thinking process of the brain enables you to access new, creative ideas that you would simply miss if you were to try to write your ideas down in a monotonous, linear fashion. Mind maps mimic your brain's thought process and help your brain fire out associations and make great leaps of understanding and imagination.

So, if you want to make an impact, start using mind maps. Every single brain has the capacity for genius!

To start you out in the right direction, here's a list of possible audiences—beyond the potential customer. It is by no means an exhaustive list but, hopefully, it will help you as you start to generate ideas:

- **Current Clients or Existing Shoppers.** Sometimes, in the quest to garner new customers, it's easy to forget about existing ones. You don't want to turn a repeat customer off because your message is only for "new" people. Amazon has built their business model on this concept; they're the master of personalization. Your method doesn't have to be that elaborate, of course, but it should take loyal, repeat customers into consideration.

- **Geographically Disparate Users.** Are you just speaking to people in your local area or worldwide? Do you sell to Canada or Mexico? If you are going to appeal to an audience outside of the Unite States, you should have materials available in that group's language or Google's translate tool at the ready.

- **Dealers or Distributors.** If you're in manufacturing, keep in mind that potential retailers will likely be checking you out online before doing business with you.

- **Alliances.** Find a way to appeal to other businesses that are complementary to yours. If you create a welcoming atmosphere, open to alliances, it can be a win/win.

- **Competitors.** There's nothing you can do to stop it: competitors *will* look at your website. As such, you may want to take certain safeguards, depending on your industry. For instance, if one of your advantages is having great product photography, you may want to watermark your images.

- **Press or Public Relations Agents.** If someone's looking to interview an expert or report on your company, you must have enough information to make that person's job as easy as possible (see Tip 8). The media looks for ready-to-go materials. To that end, make things downloadable and be sure to have:

  - An overview that includes a corporate profile and current locations.

  - A backgrounder that gives the company's history.

  - Photos, charts, graphs, or illustrations that help tell your company's story.

- Brief bios and headshots of the company's key officers and spokespersons.

Want Extra Credit?

Now that you've brain-stormed out your audience, create personas for them using the iOS app "Personas" for the iPad, like I discussed in Chapter 1.

- Bulleted fact sheets about products or services.
- Testimonials or reviews.
- Links to other sites or articles that have any editorial mentions of your company.
- Recent press releases.
- A list of frequently asked questions about your company.
- Marketing collateral or brochures.

- **Potential Employees.** As your business grows, you'll be continuously looking for the best possible talent. Your site needs to appeal to top-tier job seekers.
- **Investors.** Not only will individual investors check out your site, so will banks and commercial lenders. Make sure you put your best foot forward. Maintaining a thorough press area and an active area for job openings will create an air of success. (There's a huge power to "subliminal messages" that are a result of appealing to one particular audience while addressing other audience members.)
- **Executives.** Last (but certainly not least), you'll need to impress your higher-ups internally. These people will inevitably be looking to see how good *they* look on the site. To this end, you may want to spruce up the bios and headshots.

All of these pieces of your mind map will tell a story. The message may be slightly different, depending on which audience member comes to your website, but the site as a whole should still tell a cohesive story.

Tip 13 Gather Assets, Including Testimonials

We hear about "assets" all the time in business. But what the heck are they? And why do they matter? Well, first off, we're not talking about "current" assets (like cash or inventory) or "long-term assets" (like your laptop or filing cabinets). On the contrary, we're talking about more intangible assets—marketing assets and more.

So, let's start with a definition from BusinessDictionary.com: An "asset" is anything that "an entity owns, benefits from, or has use of, in generating income."

Assets can come as physical items on your balance sheets or in new, modern ways. If you have a website that you're not constantly loading fresh content into, for example, it will simply begin to depreciate—just like that stupid PC-Load-Letter-error-message-riddled printer you're still keeping on your balance sheet.

Let's just look at eight different, possible types of marketing assets, and which ones might be important to you:

1. **Written Assets.** Copy-related assets include all of the persuasive content, sales information, web copy, blogs, and written materials that you use to market your products, inform the public (like press releases), relate your brand to the marketplace, and describe who you are and what you do.

2. **Photographic Assets.** These types of assets include the visuals that accompany copywriting and images. This can encompass anything, from staff photos to product shots to candids from your cell phone (e.g., lifestyle photos and casual pics).

3. **Video Assets.** Video assets include commercials, of course, but also extend to customer service videos, how-to videos, YouTube clips, product videos, and promotional files. Do yourself a favor and separate raw footage and B-roll (shots that set the scene for the story you're trying to tell) from your final files.

4. **Marketing Assets.** Anything from PDF versions of print collateral to one-page fact sheets about your products would all be included here. Brochures and catalogs are just a couple of examples.

5. **Social Assets**. Your Tweets, Facebook posts, podcasts, Instagram insights—everything that you use to connect what you do to the outside world—all build engagement, trust, and inbound links to your website. Don't forget about user-generated content; anything that your customers write (or photograph) about you or your products (including reviews, rants, and raves) can be studied and repurposed.

6. **Graphic Assets.** This comprises everything from your company logos and infographics to charts and other data-related materials and graphs. This also includes logos in vector formats (so they can be resized without becoming fuzzy), as well as web-ready graphic-formatted files (like transparent background PNGs and JPGs).

7. **E-commerce Assets.** This type of asset lives in its own world, consisting mainly of spreadsheets to track all things product-related (from item names and numbers to short and long product descriptions). All of that crucial information, kept in manageable documents (along with standardized photos and uniform backgrounds) makes up the majority of e-commerce assets.

8. **Customer Testimonials.** Though this may not seem like the others, this is one of the most important assets you have. Shoppers are more persuaded by other customers' testimonials— which also includes product reviews—than by any other marketing message. According to a study by Dimensional Research, a whopping 90 percent of respondents said that positive online reviews influenced their buying decisions.[2] Great reviews make for great testimonials, whereas negative feedback sorts out the issues that *aren't* working, and makes your process better overall—that is, of course, if you're consistently listening and refining.

Once you have a fair grasp of which assets you hold in each of these areas, you will be able to see the widescreen view of where your company has been and where it's going next. Make a commitment to establishing a set of standards when it comes to how you identify and manage your intangible assets.

You need to have storage space (lots of it, probably, if you use video)—whether in hard drives, in the cloud, or at an off-site facility. Files must be named clearly, filed logically, and organized. This is especially important as you add new content.

Your staff will need to be able to access files easily—but don't just give away the keys to the kingdom. Be selective about who can see and use your assets, or they might "go missing"—just like that box of highlighters you can't seem to find.

So, how is a logo different from a lawnmower as a physical asset to a landscaping business? Well, in terms of value, it's not. If identified and managed correctly, *any* type of asset can become a life beacon for your business. You just have to notice them!

The idea here is really to expand your perception of what an asset is and can be, and figure out new and innovative ways to function in an asset-gathering mode all the time, especially among people making contact with customers, interacting with them, or processing consumer feedback.

Today's assets are not just on your balance sheet. They are deemed to have real value to your business and, if you can be aware of them and gather them, you will boost your bottom line automatically.

(Don't miss Tip 38, which explains how to use Dropbox as your "digital asset locker.")

Tip 14 Fine-Tune the User Experience

"Your website should be user-friendly!" Everyone has heard that, but what does that mean exactly? Well, it's really hard to define in a *non-technical* way. There's a deeply technical side of usability—information architecture, IT, and more—and those things are certainly legitimate. Overall, though, it's about giving people the freedom to do what they want to do.

Essentially, if your site is truly user-friendly, then your user doesn't have to think. Navigating your site and participating in your call to action should be an intuitive, organic process. It's not necessarily about the KISS principle (keep it simple, stupid); you *can* have a complex site—as long as you don't make the visitor think too hard to use it.

At this point, we need to look at what truly makes your site *different*. You know you can't be all things to all people, and on the flip side, you can't have one big button that users can push to get their desired result. Ultimately, you have to understand what your various users want, and how to give it to them—efficiently, effectively, and easily.

If you read Tips 11 and 12, then you understand who you are and have determined what kind of success you want to get from your site. Now, you need to remove any roadblocks from your site that may stand in the way of that success. Start with these steps.

1. Create an ease of use before a visitor even reaches your website. Try your best to:

   • Choose a URL that is easy to say and easy to spell.

   • Get a dot com (as opposed to a dot net or other extension, unless you are a tech startup that can get away with a clever misspelling and .ly!).

2. Make sure that visitors can quickly assess who you are, what it is that you do, and what you have to offer. This is true of every page of your site, not just your homepage (because search engines often direct people to pages *within* your site first). Consider the following:

   • Make sure your company name and logo are prominently placed. Based on eye-tracking studies, the upper left is the correct placement.

   • Include a tagline that explains what your company does.

   • Have a page header that makes clear what it is that you're selling.

   • Ensure that your typeface is large enough to read (even on mobile devices).

3. Build trust. Many site owners expect that visitors will simply take them at face value: "We have a website, so that means

we're legitimate." People are more skeptical and scared than that, though. They need to have a good feeling about someone they're about to do business with. It all comes down to trust.

- Include real testimonials that are context-specific. If you let your best advocates tell the story for you on the pages where you want users to take action, it can lead to more sales.

- Make sure you have a solid "About Us" section that emphasizes your legitimacy and presence in the "real world" (instead of just in cyberspace).

- List your full address and phone number.

- Add pictures of your building and/or employees.

- Create a trust statement (i.e., "We are the most trusted source for _____.").

4. Create a call to action. Be clear about what particular thing you want users to *do* once they come to your site.

    - Determine your points of interaction (i.e., search box for an informational site, checkout button for an e-commerce site, etc.) and make sure that they're easy to access.

    - When leading a user into a checkout, registration, or download process, remove any distractions or extraneous information.

    - Buttons should be large enough and legible enough, and need to indicate that they are to be clicked.

5. Make it easy for your users to access the content they're looking for. By doing this, you're saying to someone, "Hey, your time is really valuable, so I'm going to make it easy for you to get what you need on my website quickly."

    - Give visual cues, paths, and enticements in order to make a person's experience *almost* thought-free.

    - Employ "bread crumbs" (or a tiered system of menus, if you have a ton of content) so that users can easily navigate.

6. Write your content in a way that is easily scannable.

- Provide clear titles.
- Utilize subheadings.
- Use numbered or bullet pointed lists.
- Bold important words.
- Make hyperlinks stand out from the rest of the text.

Once you've done all of these things, observe a new visitor. A great way to test your site's usability is to sit behind someone who's never been to your site before and watch him or her click around. Notice where your user goes and how he or she gets there. Don't point things out or help the person to navigate. Just observe.

You are likely to be surprised about how people use your site. It's natural to assume that your site is intuitive and easy to use. Keep in mind, though, that someone visiting your site for the first time doesn't know what you know. The things that you think are "obvious" may not be to your average user. After your observation, ask yourself the following questions.

- Was it easy for your visitor to get to what he or she wanted to get to?
- Were site elements located where your visitor expected them to be?
- Was the visitor slow to navigate the homepage (i.e., was he or she overwhelmed by the amount of content or options)?

Why is gauging your site's user-friendliness an important exercise? Well, we know from user behavior that if your site is not scannable and easily understood within the first few seconds, they'll click elsewhere. So, paying attention to those first few seconds should be a priority.

Once you get deeper into this exercise, it may be easy to get distracted by issues further down in your website. It's important to note these, but it's even more important to prioritize them. Pay attention to those first few seconds, and then attend to the rest of your list.

What the Research Says
With Dr. Norah Dunbar

Chapter 3 is focused on your online presence and the messages that you send with your company's website. Researchers have been investigating for some time whether interactivity on a website helps or hinders the persuasiveness of the message. Interactivity is really about making communication with customers two-way, giving them active control over their experience, and improving the responsiveness of the website. If the website has too many bells and whistles, however, it can be distracting to customers. Even so, interactivity also conveys credibility.

A research study led by Guohua Wu at California State University Fullerton and published in the *Journal of Computer-Mediated Communication* explored this very issue. They found a strong relationship between customers' perceptions of interactivity and their initial perceptions of the trustworthiness of the website.[3]

The study suggested:

1. Online vendors should make their website welcoming. Customers should feel like guests, so a website should be built with customers' needs and desires in mind.

2. Websites should be in the control of the user. By breaking information into smaller chunks and letting customers navigate it, you enhance the customer's sense of control over the pace and rhythm of their interaction.

3. The website should have the responsiveness we are accustomed to in face-to-face communication. That means every keystroke or mouse movement should have an immediate response—even if it's something simple (like text that changes color as you mouse over it). If you can be more elaborate and incorporate features like a live chat with a human, you can really make customers feel welcome.

Tip 15 Learn About SEO or Hire Someone Who Already Gets It

Your website is great—once users are there. But how do you get visitors to come to it? The number-one complaint business owners tend to have is "People can't find me online. How the heck do I get listed on Google?" Considering that organic search is the number-one way people find out about new business, these business owners have their priorities right.

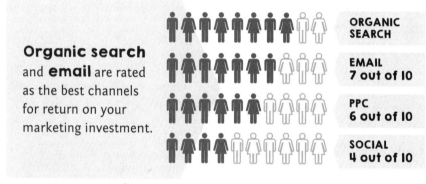

Organic search and **email** are rated as the best channels for return on your marketing investment.

ORGANIC SEARCH

EMAIL
7 out of 10

PPC
6 out of 10

SOCIAL
4 out of 10

SOURCE: CONDUCTOR®

Well, it's not so much a question of getting *listed* on Google, which is actually pretty easy to do. You can submit your site or simply wait for it to be "crawled" by "bots" (which happens more quickly than you might think).

So, the real question isn't "How do I get listed?" but rather, "What can I do to appear on the *first page* of returned search results for phrases that are being frequently searched?"

The key to search engine optimization (SEO) is "playing ball" within Google's ranking algorithms. The problem is that you can't really learn the rules of the game. Google not only keeps its algorithms secret, it is also constantly changing them. It's nearly impossible to guess all factors Google is using (at any given time) to index and rank pages. The good news is that you don't need to know all of them. You just need to know enough of what it takes to rank well for a given phrase, in relation to how your competitors rank in comparison.

An important part of Google's algorithms have to do with forces *outside* of your website, mainly based on engagement, and include:

- Activity on other Google properties Youtube and Google+.
- Your social media outposts, Facebook, Twitter, etc.
- Positive reviews of your business on Yelp, Google Local, and the like.
- Inbound links—the more reputable source, the better.

The external factors are weighed differently based on the competition for the phrase. For instance, the first result on Google for the highly competitive phrase "class-action lawyer" needs a lot more external engagement and credibility than a "long tail" phrase for a specific niche, such as "bungee jumping Los Angeles." Niche search words with qualifiers, such as location and other descriptors, "grow the tail" into a very specific phrase.

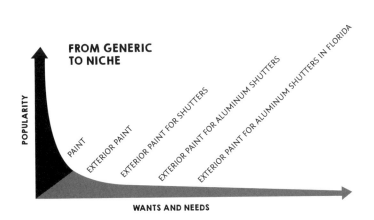

Long tail phrases by their very nature are specific and have a higher probability of leading to a sale than their generic counterparts. I am going to keep the external parts of the ranking at bay for now; this particular tip has to do specifically with your website and the things that you can do *internally* to have a search-engine friendly site.

Because of the mystery of Google's processes, three distinct camps have emerged in the SEO game. One is the "best practices" camp and another is the "game the system" camp. We'll look briefly at each and then examine a third option available to you: hiring a high-end SEO provider.

Best Practices

Building a search engine–friendly website starts with a site that is user-friendly. Search engines look at metrics such as time on site to determine the user's engagement with your website. If someone hits their back button to look further into the original search engine results page (SERP), it will be assumed that the user did not find what they needed. Websites that engage the user to go deeper and not go back to the SERP are viewed as most valuable.

"There are tons of misconceptions and fallacies about rankings," warns Steve Kinney of Search Optimizers. "The 'Field of Dreams' fallacy is that, if you build it—and do the right things—then you'll get a great ranking. Best practices do make a site search-engine-friendly. Unfortunately, SEO isn't a 'one-and-done' kind of thing."

The "best practices" camp advocates making your content easy to read in a human, natural way. Your text needs to be relevant to the topic at hand, legible, and easily scannable, and must somehow tell a story (instead of just being a jumble of keywords).

Of course, that's not always easy to do. So, I've prepared a list of Do's and Don'ts.

Do:

- Create engaging content that encourages your readers to stay a while.
- Use keyword-rich text.
- Include brand names and keywords *as text* (as opposed to embedding them as images).
- Aim for more than 250 words on each page, but don't go overboard.
- Give pages unique titles that are relevant to each page's content.
- Make headings for each page within <h1> (header) tags.
- Give images descriptive alt tags.
- Do your best to stay within WC3 web standards (and check your HTML by going to *http://validator.w3.org*).

- List your business with Google Local and Internet yellow pages (see Tips 32 and 33).
- Get inbound links from reputable sources.

Don't:

- Include graphics or images without alt tags.
- Use the same title tag (or a bad title tag) on all pages of the site.
- Use text sparingly; less is not necessarily more.
- Use text that you can't highlight or cut and paste. (Be aware of what appears to be text but is actually an image.)
- Repeat your keywords in a way that is not narrative or natural.

That's a great start, but let's have a reality check. Even the specific phrase "Huntington Beach surf schools" returns over 84,000 results. For your surf business to be listed on page one, you are either buying an ad, which may cost you upwards of $5+ per click, or you would need to be in the top .01 percent organically. Search engine–friendly alone is unlikely to get you to the coveted top of the results.

How do you know if you're using the right keywords? Ultimately, you need to:

1. Answer the question of what your content is about. Sometimes, what you're actually saying is different than your overall topic. In other words, there may be keywords associated with your content that don't actually appear on your page. One little trick is to go to Quintara.com and use your keywords as search terms to see what else comes up in the related term's "cloud."

2. See what kind of demand there is for your particular keywords (versus related terms) and figure out who your competition is for those keywords. You can actually find these things out rather easily by going to SEMRush.com.

"If you have a niche enough market and you feel that you can do these search engine–friendly checklists and get highly ranked, then you're one of the 4 percent of sites that can do so," says Kinney. "But, even so, you have to watch your step and watch your back; you can lose ground quickly and easily."

Link Labeling

When other sites link to yours, Google considers them "inbound links." When you link to another website, it's called an "outbound link." Inbound links are one of your biggest assets!

Inbound links are an important part of Google's algorithm. Google is all about quality, relevance, and context of links—not quantity (as in: the number of times you use a keyword, the number of "spam type" sites that link back to you, etc.). When people link to your content organically, because they view your stuff as useful, Google gives that more weight than anything you could generate through mass listing.

A site's rank in a search engine is, in fact, determined by the quantity and quality of inbound links. That said, Google has stated in the past that "page rank is one of over 200 signals that can affect how your site is crawled, indexed and ranked."[4] In other words, inbound links are not the end all and be all. Nonetheless, if you want deeper information about the sites that are linking to yours, go to OpenSiteExplorer.org.

Game the System

Because it's not easy to boost search rankings through best practices alone, a host of so-called "black hat" (read: violating the published "rules" of the search engines; search support.google.com for the newest list) techniques have been designed to trick the search engines into ranking a page higher.

The fact is, if you've read articles with "tricks" for boosting your ranking—and they're more than six months old—they're kind of irrelevant. That information has been out there long enough that people have already been using those "tricks." You might have just started learning about SEO, but all of the good "tricks" that are out there have already been absorbed. Beyond "tricks" becoming irrelevant, some of the stuff was wrong (or ineffective) the day it was written, and some may be just plain shady advice, resulting in penalties from search engines.

There are "black hat" SEO companies that are very comfortable operating in the gray area of what Google allows (Google may turn a blind eye at first because Google often makes money on these iffy sites). Regardless of what Google's official line is, there will always be people who continue to see if they can get away with more. The fact is, black hat companies that cheat the system, often get away with it—for a period of time.

Someone using these kinds of black hat techniques might try to manipulate content by:

- Employing "keyword stuffing." (Some companies put long lists of keywords on their site—and not much else.)

- Loading the source code with keywords. (Search engines search source code. So, some companies put search terms in their comments tags, so that they will be crawled.)

- Using invisible text. (Some web designers format keywords in a text color that matches the background color so that they aren't visible to visitors, but are readable by spiders.)

In addition, black hatters may focus on links by:

- Engaging in "content scraping." A site may pull/steal content from other sites in order to appear to have original, relevant content.

- Developing "link farms." The sole purpose of this network of webpages and websites is to link back to other sites.

- Creating "doorway pages." These nonfunctional pages and sites link to a site, but aren't intended for a visitor to see. They are created just so that search engines will index the site higher.

Because there are layers upon layers of confusion when it comes to SEO (beyond the obvious "buy links" e-mail that will inevitably appear in your inbox), it can be difficult to spot a "black hat" company. Many of them even say, "We don't use any illegal techniques!" Well, *none* of the iffy techniques are illegal; they're just ineffective in the long run.

The classic example of a SEO scandal is JC Penney. The retailer's SEO company was using black hat techniques (i.e., link buying), which eventually got figured out. When that happened, tens of thousands of the retailer's key phrases that *had* been ranked #1, overnight, turned into #75—or worse.

Luckily, there are two other ways to go beyond joining one of these two camps.

Pay for Results

Search engines exist to give you a set of results based on which keywords you type in. Your website can be listed higher up on that search results page—for a price. All search engines place paid results at the top of their search listings. Some search engines are clearer about what constitutes a paid result versus an unpaid result ("organic"). Google prides itself on differentiating the types of listings it returns in its search results. On other search engines, it's not always so clear.

Some businesses always feel like they need to be in the "paid" game—and it can be an important piece of an online marketing budget. If it's the only way you're going, however, you'll probably find that your budget must increase over time just to keep you in the same spot. This, among other reasons, is why companies supplement their budgets to include employing a SEO company.

Hire an Expert

If you're not interested in paying for placement, or you want to appear on the first page organically *as well as* in pay-for-play, then your best bet is to hire a high-end SEO company.

What's the difference between high-end SEO and regular SEO? The former will give you a customized strategy, as opposed to the latter, which is likely to simply follow a set of checklists. In that regard, high-end SEO rolls out slowly, perpetually evolves, and continues on with increasing momentum. It's strategic, precise, and methodical.

High-end SEO takes a look at what your likelihood is, over time, of being well-ranked for certain key phrases that are actually being searched for. A team of analysts looks at a series of equations to see if you're within the norms (search engine credibility), and then fine-tunes the process, based on advanced techniques.

High-end SEO utilizes a very methodical approach to even pick where to *start*. It mathematically takes a look at where you sit in your market—among your competitors—and makes sure that you're in a good part of the bell curve. (Being an outlier is not a good thing in this case.)

"It's not *one* bell curve," notes University of California–Irvine SEO Instructor and Search Optimizers CEO Steve Kinney, "but hundreds—  based on each phrase. It's tiny little analyses. In some regard, it's like the Olympic decathlon. You may not win any one individual sport, but all added up, you can win the overall event."

The goal is to go with core phrases that can gain a small amount of momentum that, eventually, gain larger momentum. You should begin to see initial results in a few weeks, but like a train gaining speed, it can take many months to go full steam into dramatic results. "You're always moving forward or moving back," explains Steve Kinney. "It's a dynamic process. Continuous effort is required so that you don't lose footing, but it also opens doors to more and better phrases over time."

It's not always easy to tell the difference between regular and high-end SEO companies at first glance. When you're trying to decide which SEO company to go with, the basis for comparison should really be accomplishments (i.e., higher rankings) versus just activities (i.e., all of the strategies employed to get there). Any high-end SEO company will be willing to "show you the money"—not just the bells and whistles. That means showing results over time and references from satisfied clients.

"You should have high expectations for your SEO company," advises Kinney. "Eventually, search should be your lowest cost form of lead generation—and it should continue to get better over time. You should expect to see a positive return on investment within a year. By 18 to 24 months, that return should accelerate even more. If it's not gaining momentum, then it's not being done effectively."

In the Real World: Northern Parrots

Thanks to WhichTestWon.com, I discovered the test case site Northern Parrots. "As the leading UK retailer of food, toys, and accessories for parrots—with a seven digit annual turnover—[NorthernParrots.com was] already

> ### Heat Map
>
> This graphical representation of data displays individual values as different colors. On the web, heat maps are often used to show which areas of a webpage are most frequently viewed by visitors. (See ChunkofChange.com/bookgoodies for a heat map example.)

getting outstanding results, thanks to e-commerce best practices and expert recommendations."[5]

Even so, with a desire to see even more stellar results, they decided to engage in split testing and saw a jump of nearly 35 percent from their first test alone. Split testing is a simple, randomized experiment that utilizes two variants (A and B): the control and the treatment. In web design, the goal is to identify changes to web pages that effect a "desired action" (such as a click-through).

Upon using a combination of tools and techniques, the testing team found that:

1. According to a "heat map," the majority of homepage clicks were performed on the side navigation, which listed product categories.

2. Although users wanted to browse, rather than search, the side navigation didn't allow for that kind of behavior.

3. Finally (which comes as no shock to us), there was no clearly identified UVP, explaining why a prospect should buy from Northern Parrots instead of a competitor's site.

"Traditional conversion funnel analysis and recommendations from experts had led the client to believe that the homepage was performing well...however, our voice-of-customer evidence suggested otherwise."

The hypotheses for this split test were clear:

A. Presenting users with a clear path to products that are relevant to them will increase conversion rate.

B. A clear UVP will increase conversion, when visitors understand why they should buy from Northern Parrots specifically.

C. Aligning the top navigation with profitable conversion paths will result in higher revenue per visitor (RPV).

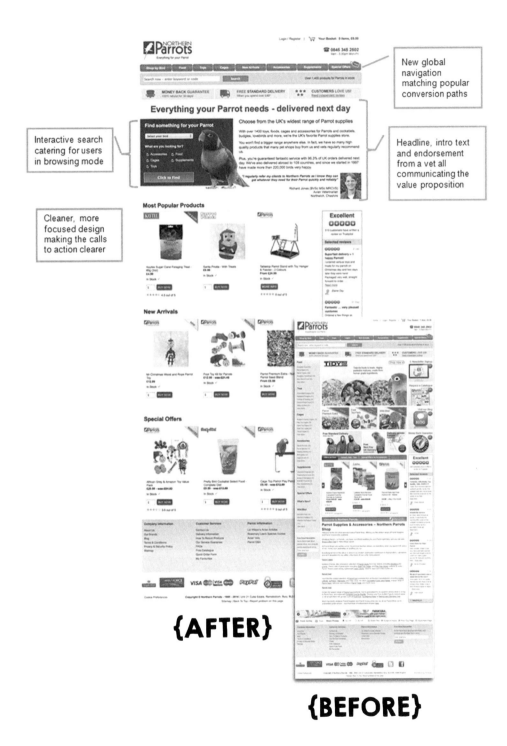

{AFTER}

{BEFORE}

AWA created a new test page, to be run for three weeks, that:

- Decluttered the design.
- Rewrote key content.
- Catered to browsers (instead of just searchers).
- Incorporated a testimonial from a veterinarian.

As you might expect, the variation outperformed the original site—to the tune of a 21 percent– to 34 percent–increase in revenue per visitor!

Don't: Put up an "Under Construction" page.

Do: Put up at least one page that projects your image and broadcasts to the world what it is that you do.

It's a mistake that people make all the time, every day, but a "Coming Soon" page is the equivalent of going out in your underwear. It's better to have one page that has your address, phone number, and logo—the very basics. Your unfinished site will simply serve as an online business card until you're ready to go live.

Even if you fully intend to update the site ASAP, remember that things can be done in phases. For instance, if you have a Spanish language audience, you don't need to translate the entire site into Spanish right away. You should, however, have at least one page that lets them know who to contact for Spanish language assistance or information.

I've placed examples of good one-pagers at ChunkofChange.com/bookgoodies. Let me know if I should add yours.

Chapter 4

Change Your Analytics

Measuring With Meaning

Rest assured: "analytics" isn't nearly as boring or dry as it sounds at first. In this chapter, I hope to take the glaze off your eyes when it comes to "analysis," which is really just so much fancy talk for gaining some insight from the information you've gathered. To succeed, it's best to keep things simple, but smart.

A (Very) Brief History of "Analytics"

In the early days of the web (read: the olden days of the 1990s), the terms "analytics" and "testing" were unheard of. Only techies with specialized knowledge would bother combing through a web server's log files in order to obtain baseline data. With that information in hand, a progressive company *might* pay a programmer thousands of dollars in order to come up with

> "Big data is like teenage sex. Everyone says they're doing it, but very few are; those that are don't do it very well."
>
> —Mike Burton, VP of Madison Logic

a basic way to test a few of their website elements. Even so, those instances were rare. Most design and functionality changes were based on instinct and personal preference.

Then came the 2000s and information overload. "You want data? We have data!" But, to what end? Managers weren't sure what, exactly, to look at. "What measurements are relevant?" they'd ask. "Which numbers are valid?" they'd wonder. Above all, they would want to know, "What does all

> ### Optimization
>
> Using data collection, analysis, and testing to continually improve your business. Keenly aware that we all have limited resources (of time, money and information), "optimization" is not "maximization." (More on that in Tip 49.) Think about:
>
> 1. Your overall business goals, as these will serve as your North Star, guiding your optimization efforts.
> 2. Measurable markers that correlate to success of those goals.
> 3. Ways to improve those markers, all of which you can test to discover what works best for your business.

of this data *tell* us?" Companies began to make changes to their sites based on their newfound mountains of data, but their efforts tended to be unfocused and haphazard. (It was the "let's try this and see what happens to the stats" approach.)

At first, most data was the result of "log-based analytics." In other words, a web server would note each and every request for each and every type of file that it served and produce a report detailing all of those activities. Then, third-party providers started giving little pieces of code that companies could embed in their websites in order to track them in a way that would provide for easier analysis. With "script-based analytics," tracking became an off-site event.

Through time, this third-party method has become the more widely used form of tracking. That doesn't mean that companies like WebTrends are dead, though. There are a lot of businesses (e.g., banks, healthcare providers, companies with military clearance, etc.) that *can't* use third-party tracking of any sort, and so they have to utilize in-house solutions based on information from their own server's logs.

The Age of Analytics Ubiquity

With the rise of third-party solutions, analytics technology has become more standardized, open to the masses, and, best of all, free to implement. Although the term "website analytics" didn't even exist before 2006, we have quickly launched into a new era—especially in terms of understanding how people interact with websites.

Essentially, a visitor to a website "votes" with his or her mouse. He or she chooses where to click and what to click and, as a result, either ends up taking an action that either benefits the website owner (e.g., a sale, a filled out form, etc.) or doesn't (e.g., exiting the site, leaving blanks on a form, etc.).

Large companies invest major money and human resources into shaping customers' behavior in a way that positively contributes to their bottom line. In order to steer users toward taking a desired action, companies monitor their websites by:

- Looking at a user's series of mouse clicks.
- Making assumptions about that user's behavior based on those clicks.
- Then implementing changes to their websites in order to increase the likelihood of the user taking that elusive desired action.

You, Too, Can Take Advantage of This Special Offer!

If the big wigs at Corporate America, Inc., can play this game, why can't you? Every business of every size can benefit from this type of optimization. The key is finding the right solutions to fit your unique business needs.

Again, the whole concept of digital data gathering and analysis can seem daunting. But that's why I'm here to break it down without the overwhelming and largely unnecessary techno-babble. Instead, we'll keep it simple and straightforward, with an eye on giving you useful steps:

- Getting into a measuring mindset.
- Setting up automated data measuring tools, such as Google Analytics.
- Deciding on the most meaningful measurements to meet your overarching goals.
- Putting data collection and analysis into action through website testing.
- Incorporating these actions into your overall business culture.

Tip 16 Get a Case of the "What Ifs"

Optimization cannot begin until you cultivate your sense of curiosity. So, that's where we'll begin.

What is the story you tell yourself about the future of your business? How can that story lead to improvement? Think big, think small, think anywhere in between. But make it a point to regularly have a *Matrix*-style moment, pausing the action in your business universe and zooming in to examine it. When you occasionally take the time to stop going about business as usual, your mind will start teeming with questions in no time at all.

Transform "What If" Into a True/False Statement

Take your curiosity and "What Ifs" and let them lead you to a true/false statement about your business.

- By asking, "What if I used the local chamber event to qualify leads?" You may be making the following statement: "If I get more qualified leads, I'll close more business."

- By asking, "What if I featured a video of the new product rolling out next month on the homepage?" You may get to this statement: "If I put the new product on the homepage, I'll get more questions about the product."

- By asking, "What if I found a complementary, not competing, product offering to bundle my unique chocolates with?" You may conclude, "If I partner with the 'organic' florist, I'll sell more of my vegan chocolates."

Hypothesis and Hype

What all the previous bullets have in common has more to do with seventh grade science lab than what is normally top of mind for business people. They all lead to a statement that can be proven true or false, which originates from a guess. And it seeks to explore what may move the needle specifically for their business. In other words: a hypothesis.

By distilling your dreamy "what if" ideas into statements (that can ultimately be rendered true or false), you are positioning yourself into smartly proving or disproving these guesses in the future. How is this done? Start by observation, then write down those observations over time.

For example, are you tracking your outbound sales follow-up after the chamber event on a spreadsheet? (See Tip 30 on how to structure such a spreadsheet.) If not, how will you truly know if the event was worth going to in the first place? You may know subjectively, by gut feel (and most people stop there). But if you don't take the extra step of looking at some objective measurements, it'll be difficult to scale up.

I'm assuming that you already have a goal in mind when you are forming your "what ifs." I talked about defining success way back in Tip 11. Now, I'm going to expand out from that to bring a curiosity culture into your business that allows for upward success.

Tip 17 Data as an All-You-Can-Eat Buffet: You Can Always Go Back for More Later

Now that you've got a case of the "what ifs," where to begin? The best (and easiest) place to start looking for signs that you're on the right path is your website. Once you understand it in the context of the web, you will find that you will start to think of "optimization" with other indicators in your business.

Therefore, if you're not already capturing your website data, then that's where you need to begin. It's the best way to start making informed decisions about changes to your site. More than 80 percent of the top 1,000 websites track user behavior—and *you* should be, too. Don't feel bad, though, if you're not already on the analytics bandwagon. It's never too late to get started and it's much easier than you think!

Google Analytics: A Good Place to Start

Start with Google Analytics; there isn't a more well-known or universally accepted free tool for measurement out there. (In fact, as of 2010, it was estimated that nearly 50 percent of the top one million websites used Google Analytics.) There are countless other providers out there (including

The validity of the data you end up getting back is dependent on the technology you choose to use. It's not at all unusual for different tracking technologies to vary wildly in the results they return. For a more detailed look at this, check out the Imulus/insights blog (at http://imulus.com/blog/2010/12/), where one writer looks at the significant divergence in results returned by four individual providers.

ones with free tools that rival Google's). That said, there isn't *any* technological tool that is 100 percent valid or reliable; there are pros and cons to each.

Of course, you should be aware of the "hidden cost" of using *any* free tool, which is the confidentiality of your data (or lack thereof). With Google Analytics, the upside is that you're getting a great product for free. The downside is that, once you use it, Google will have access to all of your site statistics—a mountain of information that it will use to improve and sell its own products. In the interest of introducing the truly uninitiated to the most universal, turnkey solution currently available, I have chosen to advocate the use of Google Analytics because of its wide acceptance, cost (which is to say, *no* cost), and ease of use.

First, you'll need to sign up for a free account by going to *www.google.com/analytics/*. You will be given directions on how to paste a required piece of script into your site's code in order to start tracking data. Once you're set up and have started tracking all of the different kinds of actions visitors are taking on your site, you'll need to figure out what to do with all the data you collect. In the next Tip, I'll explain just how to go about measuring the right things and how to best use the information you gather.

From Data to Analytics: Figure Out What You Are Really Measuring

Once you're tracking and measuring the statistics on your site, it's very easy to get overwhelmed, hone in on the wrong things, and end up with that dreaded analysis paralysis condition. Luckily, it's not terminal.

Google Analytics is just a name; the analytics part implies analysis, or what gives data meaning. Therefore, most businesses stop at what "analysis" Google gives them, but, fail to question whether those indicators are actually meaningful.

	Source / Medium	Sessions	Sessions	Contribution to total: Sessions
		52,945 % of Total: 100.00% (52,945)	52,945 % of Total: 100.00% (52,945)	
1.	■ google / cpc	29,320	55.38%	
2.	■ google / organic	9,827	18.56%	
3.	■ (direct) / (none)	3,968	7.49%	
4.	google.com / referral	2,581	4.87%	
5.	■ yahoo / organic	1,746	3.30%	
6.	bing / organic	1,006	1.90%	
7.	■ admissions.calbar.ca.gov / referral	822	1.55%	
8.	en.wikipedia.org / referral	264	0.50%	
9.	hg.org / referral	160	0.30%	

In other words, Google Analytics does do some analysis via fancy math that gets you to stats like unique visitors, and it stops there. To take what you get from Google Analytics in order to make informed business decision requires another step: the actual analysis.

It's not uncommon to hear an executive, new to analytics, say something like, "Oh my God! We have a page that just spiked in its 'bounce rate.' What do we do?!?" Often, that person has overlooked an important detail, such as the fact that the terrible-bounce-rate-page happens to be the "thank you" page, where visitors are *expected* to leave the site. (In this case, obviously, that particular metric is not a good measurement of performance.)

Avoid the Allure of Sticky Statistics

There's an undeniable allure to big numbers that *seem* like impressive stats. That's why so many websites still report the number of hits they receive, even though the measurement of hits is outdated and relatively useless.

In the beginning, there wasn't a way to know whether a customer "came through the door." By tracking hits, you could only determine that a computer somewhere was requesting data from your website. Unfortunately, a hit included every single thing that a website needed in order to properly display a page (e.g., an image, a link to a file, a script running on a page, etc.). Thus, *one* visit to a homepage that had multiple photos on it might result in five *hits*.

Despite its relative uselessness as a measurement, companies really liked the stat because it looked impressive and, therefore, stroked their egos. Although some sites hung on dearly to the notion of hits, most eventually moved on to looking at "page views." Then, after installing cookies, they began tracking "visitors" and, later, "unique visitors." Over time, however, analytics has thoroughly branched out.

Similarly, Twitter may report that it has a whopping 75+ million users. What it fails to note, however, is that only 17 percent of its users actually posted a tweet in the past month, taking some of the pluck out of the attempted puffery. In this case, you can see how counting "users" does little to measure the site's actual performance.

So keep a clear head when zeroing in on the stats that support your bottom line. These are the measures that mean something behind closed doors, the real markers of your business success—not the impressive (if opaque) PR sound bytes you strategically put front and center for the world at large. (You know, the ones three out of four dentists agree on.)

Tip 18 Make Metrics Meaningful: From Analytics to Key Performance Indicators

So, you've progressed from developing a healthy sense of curiosity to measuring information. Now, you have a spreadsheet or report showing more information than you know what to do with. Literally.

How do you now progress from a crush of pure data to meaningful information, the kind from which sound, optimization-centered business decisions can be made?

The goal of analytics is *not* to simply collect a ton of data and spit out a bunch of numbers. In fact, that's a worse case scenario than collecting no data at all. Think pragmatically about big-picture goals as you contemplate potential data-mining missions. Ideally, you want to make positive changes to your website (i.e., enhancements in design or content) and, in turn, increase your bottom line (and/or decrease costs).

So, which measurements relate the best to *your* bottom line? The three main questions you should be asking yourself are:

- What, exactly, am I measuring?
- Is that measurement important?
- If it's not important, what should I be measuring instead?

Unlocking Key Performance Indicators (KPIs)

The important measurements you will define are more commonly known as "key performance indicators" (KPIs). Like all sites, you'll probably track your page views and unique visitors. Your other KPIs, however, will vary depending on types of visitors who come to your site.

Thus, KPIs are a subset of your analytics that provide you with:

- A report that has specific meaning for your business.

- Key insights that reveal how well you are doing in reaching your goals.
- The kind of information that can be acted upon.

Hopefully, your measurements will serve as a catalyst for you to do something different—ideally, something *better*. And not just in a spastic, willy-nilly manner, but by virtue of measured data with important impact on ultimate goals. What analytics should do, ultimately, is give you *insight*.

Conversion Rate

If you only look at *one* thing, look at **conversion rate**.

Regardless of your type of business, you want your visitors to take some sort of action. Thus, you should be measuring to see if there is an increase of people taking that desired action over a period of time.

The denominator in this formula can be controversial as it depends on a keen understanding of the business goals.

"Amazon is known to measure [conversion] by session, as they consider every visit an opportunity to convert. Many retailers prefer to look at unique visitors," says Bryan Eisenberg,[1] *New York Times* best selling author of *Call to Action*, "whereas others are quick to point out that the bottom figure may need to be filtered more. For instance, if you are converting for users that sign up to be part of your database, you would need to filter out repeat users that already signed up to get a meaningful conversion statistic."

Useful KPI Examples

Some common KPIs include the percentage of new and returning visitors, a list of where your visitors are coming to your site from, as well as a site-wide conversion rate (or, how many people came versus how many people took the desired action). There are also KPIs that are specific to e-commerce sites, including:

- Sales per visitor.

- Average order value.

- Average number of items purchased.

- Shopping cart abandonment rate.

- Revenue and profit per product.

- Repeat order rate over a given period (which is used to help calculate "lifetime value").

> Avinash Kaushik offers a really good list of KPIs (among other things) on his blog, Occam's Razor. For a more detailed look at steps that an expert analyst would take, check out his blog (at *bit. ly/AKDataAnalysis*, paying attention in particular to Steps 7 and 8).

Overall, there are certain qualities that make for a truly useful KPI, including how easy it is to understand (and, in turn, communicate to management) and how helpful it is in the decision-making process. In order to identify what your particular KPIs are, ask yourself the following questions:

- Is it *key*? In other words, based on your business, is the measurement in question something that relates (either directly or indirectly) to your bottom line?

- Does it measure *performance*? Does the measurement relate to either increased revenue or decreased cost?

- Is it an *indicator*? Have you identified a consistent measurement that is capable of showing some sort of meaningful change over time?

Once you have a few months' worth of KPIs under your belt, you'll probably be able to identify some areas of concern and come up with possible solutions that you'd like to implement in order to improve. I'll explain exactly how to do this in the tip that follows.

Sample KPI Sheet for Online Retailer

	Month to Date	Projection	Prev Month	% change Month over Month
Advertising Impressions	149,355	172,208	32,532	429%
Clicks	4,742	5,538	4,390	26%
Click Thru Rate (CTR)	3.2%	3.2%	13.5%	-76%
Total Visitors	36,997.4	42,478	33,747	26%
Unique Visitors	28,713	32,967	26,531	24%
Rev Per Visitor	**2.70**	**2.70**	**2.20**	**23%**
Orders	498.3	572	311	84%
Total Revenue	**$99,775.85**	**$114,557.46**	**$74,275.13**	54%
Conversion	1.35%	1.35%	0.92%	46%
Average Order Value	$200.23	$200.23	$238.83	-16%
LTV	**$251.29**	**$251.29**	**$299.73**	-16%
Returns	**$12,463.55**	**$14,310.01**	**$11,739.27**	22%

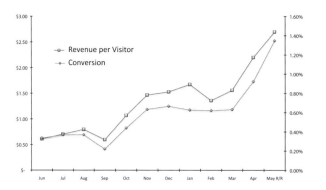

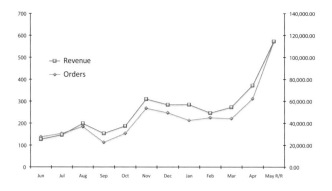

Email Revenue

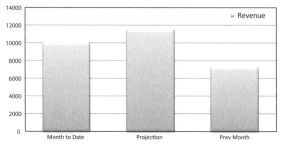

What the Research Says
With Dr. Norah Dunbar

As a researcher, understanding data is my bread and butter, so it always shocks me when I hear about people making important decisions without knowing all the facts. Buying a house, starting a business, even naming your child can have implications for a lifetime. So, why wouldn't you want to know everything you can and make your decisions in an informed way?

In your web-based business, you have a wealth of data available to you, and Olga has described well how to make sense of it to benefit your business. I thought I would also share some basic research principles to keep in mind to help you when thinking like a researcher.

1. Try to stay as objective as possible. Although you have an emotional attachment to your business, you should not be emotionally attached to your data. If your data suggests your marketing strategy is not working, then make the change you need to make. Don't argue with your data or dig in your heels.

2. Have questions to ask before you see the results. Start by asking yourself what you really want to know about your customers or your web traffic before you start looking at the analytics. One of the problems researchers have when they start getting into "big data" is that they don't know what's unexpected if they don't know what to expect. Ask your questions first and then let the answers guide you.

3. Use multiple sources of information. Don't put all your eggs in one basket. It's good advice when examining data relating to your online business. One website where you are running an advertisement might have a different customer base than another and, as a result, the analytics from one might give you different results than another. Asking customers you trust to give you feedback to confirm what you are seeing in your data, getting multiple team members to see if they are interpreting the data in the same way, or discussing your strategies for change with your key stakeholders are all ways of triangulating your results from different sources.

Tip 19 Continually Test Your Website

Once you've determined what you really want to say, who you want to say it to, and how exactly you're going to say it, you'll need to determine whether what you're saying is effective. Your website serves as the ideal testing ground, given the ease with which you can gather and view your online statistics.

Ultimately, your visitors have the final say in whether your design and messages are working in your favor. This is where testing comes in. Making website testing a standard maintenance element will dramatically affect your overall optimization efforts.

> "If you have a website, you have activities that you want your users to complete (e.g., make a purchase, sign up for a newsletter) and/or metrics that you want to improve (e.g., revenue, session duration, bounce rate). With Google Content Experiments, you can test which version of a landing page results in the greatest improvement in conversions (i.e., completed activities that you measure as goals) or metric value. You can test up to 10 variations of a landing page."
>
> —*bit.ly/AnaylticsHelp*

What Is Testing?

Essentially, what you're doing is just presenting different choices that affect your user's experience (i.e., colors, images, messages, promotions, etc.) with the goal of figuring out which things are the most effective for a specific purpose or audience.

Suppose the owner of your company says, "Nobody likes orange, so we're never going to use orange on our website." Later, however, testing shows that site users actually preferred that color (i.e., an orange page increased sales by 50 percent on one particular day). You're not one-upping the owner, then, when you recommend going with orange. All you're saying is, "Based on the testing we did, orange made more sales. So, we should go down this path."

Why Is Testing Important?

Testing can reveal how visitors use your site and what their preferences are. That kind of information can help you to make changes that optimize your website over time.

Who Is Testing "Right" For?

Don't look at testing as an "only geeks can love it" kind of thing. Ultimately, the changes that result from successful testing improve not only the website visitor's experience, but your company's bottom line, as well.

In reality, anyone interested in boosting the bottom line (and who *isn't*?) should be itching to do some testing. Either your company is progressive and already aware of the need to make improvements to its website, *or* your company isn't convinced of the need for change and, as such, you require proof that will convince management. Either way, testing is the answer.

What Does Testing Cost?

In the past few years the floodgates have really opened up for testing. Whereas previously it cost a lot of money, time, and effort to undertake meaningful testing, now there are free, web-based tools that provide easy-to-implement solutions. Cost is no longer an issue; you're only inhibited by the time you have available to devote to testing. Even if you opt for a paid method of testing, it's a very small investment compared to the resulting increase in sales. In other words, a testing firm should be able to pay for itself.

Isn't Testing Complicated?

Testing can seem like pretty scary stuff. Don't let the mathematics and graphics get you into a tizzy, though. The basics are really easy and the tools available today make the process quite manageable. The main reason that testing is viewed as challenging is that people have a very difficult time defining what they're testing.

True success in testing occurs when you tie the reason for your tests directly to your bottom line. Often, that means measuring "conversion," which is a specific goal (i.e., entering credit card information) tied to some part of the process (e.g., the shopping cart checkout) that contributes to your bottom line (i.e., final sales). To simplify, a "conversion rate" compares the number of visitors that came to your site versus the number that complete your desired action (Visitors Completing the Desired Goal/Total Visitors × 100 percent). See Tip 18, for a longer discussion on conversion.

G.H. Brooks, on blogs.keynote.com, says:

"[T]he average retail site has a conversion rate of 1–2 percent. A successful retail site has a conversion rate of 7–9 percent. A good 'lead generation' website (one where success is defined as a lead being generated for a sale, or a subscription) converts somewhere around 16–18 percent, the average site 5–6 percent."

Brooks further argues that moving the needle by one percentage point, from a 1 percent to 2 percent conversion, in a scenario where an e-commerce website has 10,000 visitors a month and an average order value of $90, equals a whopping $108,000 a year in additional revenue.

That said, try not to think of your conversion rate as a specific goal number, but rather as an indicator of progress over time.

You simply need to know what your desired result is (i.e., selling more widgets) and then reverse engineer what the process is for the user *getting to* the desired result. There are usually many desired actions along the way (i.e., find the widget, buy the widget, complete the checkout, etc.). Those steps are your testing (and optimization) opportunities.

Of course, a "desired action" will vary from website to website. For instance:

- If you're selling something on your site, your desired action is likely to be a visitor completing a purchase. ("If I put a bigger graphic on the homepage, will it lead to more people purchasing a widget?")

- If you have a service-oriented business, your desired action might be to have a visitor complete a contact form. ("If I make certain fields optional, instead of required, will it increase the number of people who fill out the form?")

- If you have a blog, your desired action might be to have a visitor stay on a page longer. ("If I lay out the content in a different way, will people spend more time on the page?")

What Kinds of Things Can We Test For?

In general, the types of pages that companies usually test are:

- Homepage.
- Landing page.
- Registration or signup page.
- Product or content page.
- Checkout or purchase page.
- Offers or promotions page.

Overall, the elements of a page that companies often experiment with include:

- Call to action.
- Page or product layout.
- Copy.
- Buttons or links.
- Headings or subheadings.
- Form fields.
- Product pictures.
- Navigation.

Ultimately, testing is an essential part of continual change and improvement. You make certain assumptions about what works and what doesn't work for your audience on your website. Testing challenges those assumptions and allows you to find out what truly performs best. This feedback loop allows you to "optimize" your site over time.

Tip 20 Bring Testing Into Your Business Culture

Incorporating data gathering, analysis, and testing into your online efforts will quickly develop your optimization skills. After that, don't be surprised if you turn into an optimization machine, with "what ifs" popping into your head—like bubbles in a bath.

Once you reach that point, you'll know you're ready to take those practices to the next level, incorporating testing into your overall business culture. Just remember to take things one step at a time, one KPI at a time, to develop processes that can be maintained over time by your available staff. Sometimes KPIs turn up in unexpected places, like YouTube.

Trial and Error Success: How the Courage Campaign Took Its Digital Spots From Zero to Hero

The Courage Campaign is a 501c(3) nonprofit grassroots advocacy organization based in California. In recent history, the organization created videos to advocate for repealing Proposition 8, California's controversial gay marriage hot button. Despite the participation of big-name entertainers, the numbers told the real deal: YouTube statistics for Courage Campaign videos showed that viewers tuned out almost immediately. Though not the original intention, the low-performing videos served as the control condition (or starting point to measure against) in a test.

Many businesses that use videos are not aware that YouTube already measures key stats beyond just "views." One of the KPIs that your business should hone in on is how long people stick around once they watch your video. This allows you to understand if they are getting your message at all.

The Courage Campaign was horrified that their original celebrity-endorsed videos lost the audience rather quickly, at only about one-third through the four-minute long video. Some huge "what ifs" popped up. What if we put more of a focus on the story of the couples that are affected (rather than celebrity endorsement)? Would that get more attention to our cause?

This case of the "what ifs" led to the true/false statement of: If we change our videos to be story focused, more people will get our message and care about our cause. The Courage Campaign hired an expert story producer with the objective of humanizing the plight of the Courage Campaign's message through authentic stories. The side-by-side results:

How Wealthy Billionaires are Trying to Destroy our Schools and Silence our Voices ⊕

Created: Oct 21, 2012 • Duration: 4:23 •

AVERAGE VIEW DURATION
1:36 (37%)

{BEFORE}

Derrence and Ed - Their Story After Ed's Passing ⊕

Created: Feb 14, 2012 • Duration: 1:10

AVERAGE VIEW DURATION
1:09 (99%)

{AFTER}

The statistics were telling. Once the new videos went up, views shot up (compared to the original videos) and, as great as that is, the more telling KPI showed that all those views got the message, sticking around until the end of the video.

Testing Tips

Test one variable at a time whenever possible. Trying out individual changes will give direct insight into how much change it alone causes. Trying two or more changes simultaneously will reflect cumulative change, making it difficult to interpret which change triggered positive or negative changes.

If one page does better than the other, you won't be able to isolate causation, the element that *triggered* the improved outcome. Was it the familiarity of the old home page design, or the addition of the "Buy It Now" button? Or were people attracted to the catchy tropical theme music on

the other page, which was so beachy-keen it transcended the absent "Buy It Now" button? So to remember this concept, just think of your brilliant, test-tastic optometrist as he puts your eyeballs through their paces, clicking down just one monocle at a time for your comparison and consideration: "Which is better? A or B? *Click, click.* Now which is better? B or C? *Click, click.* Now which is better? B or D?"

The term "success" is a bit of a misnomer here. Even if your hypothesis is not proven (i.e., the test does not achieve the desired outcome), it is still a worthwhile experiment. It will help you hone in on what the next thing to test should be. Some argue that we learn more from our failures than our successes. Creating a testing culture is a competitive advantage.

Use Your Newfound Knowledge to Take Action

Quantitative testing isn't a cure-all. Analytics by itself can only answer the "what" question. Testing often answers the "how." In order to answer the "why," though, you need to have some sort of interaction with the user (feedback form, live chat, survey, etc.) or do some form of qualitative testing (e.g., usability testing, etc.). Hopefully, the insights you gain will lead you to more "what if" questions.

Interested in different testing methodologies? Then check out some of these techniques in more detail on ChunkofChange.com/bookgoodies:

- A/B testing.
- Multi-path multivariate testing.
- Split-path testing.
- Do anything testing.
- Linger testing.
- Click testing.

In the Real World: COO Joy Cropper Puts AAA to the Test

Every business owner makes or delegates critical marketing and branding decisions on a regular basis. Although there's not an exact formula for always making the "right" choices, it's certainly possible to make much more informed decisions through information gathering, smart statistical analysis, and testing.

Meet Joy Cropper

"I graduated from Duke University in 1991 and my first job was at an ad agency working on Ocean Spray, before the Internet was even a marketing consideration," Cropper told me with a smile. "As websites and other online tactics started to become viable marketing opportunities, I volunteered to take on online projects and gradually became a specialist in online strategy, website information architecture and usability, and user research."

Cropper has worked both client side and at ad agencies through the years, previously serving as lead online strategist at J. Walter Thompson working on Ford Motor Co.'s websites, before joining Williams Randall 11 years ago, first as director of Internet strategy and now as COO, director of online services.

For additional insight on just how to accomplish this, I had the opportunity to speak with Joy Cropper of Williams Randall Marketing, an Indianapolis, Indiana, advertising and web development agency. As COO, director of online services, Cropper leads the company's web team, helps manage agency operations, and oversees measurement and analytics efforts.

Showing the true signs of a testing addict, one of the things Joy enjoys about her job is being proven wrong—in testing scenarios, at least. "I think we and our clients tend to believe that as experienced marketers, we know what's going to work," she shared. "But I love testing different ideas because the results are often unexpected."

Cultivating a Testing Culture

In addition to helping its clients implement analytics and testing goals, Williams Randall strives to regularly nourish its own in-house testing culture. "Our agency develops a list of Top 10, 'Hell or High Water' goals that we absolutely want to accomplish each year," Cropper explained. "We started by adding two specific goals about tracking and testing: (1) Report results after every campaign, and (2) Execute at least 12 marketing tests with case studies."

Though Cropper notes that results weren't instantaneous, prioritizing definitely helped: "That certainly got us started on the path of reinforcing to our staff, and ultimately our clients, that tracking, testing, and reporting is very important and needs to be planned out and budgeted for every possible project," Cropper said. "Year one of focusing on that first goal showed us that we hadn't quite gotten it right, and the next year we changed it to 'Report results during and after every campaign.' The key difference being building in the time and resources to report on efforts while they were happening so that analysis and optimization could occur before a campaign was over."

The company also continued to improve on their second goal, which, according to Cropper, served an important dual purpose: to demonstrate to current clients the impact of Williams Randall's work on their business, and also the value the company could bring to potential clients.

Winning With Surprising Results

Joy Cropper's work initially caught my eye when I saw her silver medal–winning entry in a contest, which featured a simple A/B split test experiment that Williams Randall performed for client AAA (see supporting image). In an effort to increase sign-ups, AAA tried running a sweepstakes-style hook, offering people who signed up a chance to win a gift card. Users saw an Adwords ad that took them to one of two landing pages, one with the sweepstakes offer and one without. The results proved surprising: the

Surprising Results from Testing Sweeps Offer

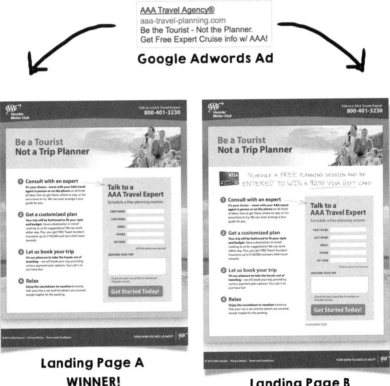

Google Adwords Ad

Landing Page A
WINNER!

Landing Page B

Results: 74% lift in form completion
Brand: AAA Hooiser Motor Club
Agency: Williams Randall Marketing
Testing Technology: Google Content Experiments

page without the sweeps offer did significantly better, to the tune of more than 70 percent more form completions.

"One main takeaway for the client was that using a sweepstakes to generate leads seemed to harm their reputation instead of entice people," said Cropper. "AAA's travel planning services are premium and the brand is well trusted by consumers; they felt that people may have perceived the contest as too gimmicky or even like a scam. Eliminating it actually increased the trust factor of the landing page." This intelligence was only gained via the test.

Begin With Baby Steps

That's great for AAA, but what about you? Joy offers excellent advice when it comes to incorporating successful testing: "I suggest walking before you run," she says. "I consider the first step in successful testing to be actually tracking and reporting." Unfortunately, Joy sees many professionals overlooking some of the simplest methods of data collection. "So many marketers aren't even putting basic tracking techniques into place."

Unfortunately, I can't boil your testing implementation down to a simple checklist. "It takes an unexpected amount of coordination and planning to make sure all the tracking details have been thought through and implemented correctly before you start a campaign," notes Cropper. Ah, the old devil in the details!

But just as with any effort to change entrenched habits, whether personal or business, committing to a consistent change in behavior can prove the biggest initial challenge. "[I]t takes commitment to actually put reports together on a regular basis," says Joy. "So I view the first step as getting that on solid ground."

"After that, I recommend picking small elements to A/B test at first," Cropper continued. "Like language or color of a button, or a different headline, or a different image. Things that are easy for the team to see and understand. Once everyone gets used to testing being a normal part of a project, put together a testing plan that outlines all the different things you want to test over the year and why. It's easy to get off track without a plan."

As a practical point, I asked about the added cost and effort running such a test, which Cropper said was fairly negligible in context. "I don't have actual figures, but it wouldn't have been a lot more than executing the campaign without a test. They invested in the SEM campaign, landing page, and results reporting no matter what. We simply added a slight variation to the SEM copy strategy, created a second version of the landing page, and reported on the results weekly."

Here are Joy Cropper's suggestions for testing tools that are accessible to small businesses:

- Unique URLs (such as for different mediums and ad creative).
- Trackable phone numbers.
- Tracking pixels (very useful and fairly easy to implement).
- Google Analytics.
- Google Content Experiments (free, easy to implement, and accessible).

Don't: Post a marketing video, then neglect to follow up on stat analysis.

Do: Examine your YouTube video stats to assess whether you're reaching your target market, and whether they're receptive to your message.

Much of this chapter focused on ways to utilize user-friendly tools to start your initial data gathering and analysis efforts. Unbeknownst to many small business owners, taking the time to check your YouTube stats can provide a virtual mother lode of invaluable information. Once you begin reading between the statistical lines, you'll have concrete data from which you can make informed optimization decisions.

Don't Ignore Valuable Video Data

Katie Covell of Sunnyland Pictures

Many business owners utilize YouTube, and a few other online providers, to post video content. This is a smart move on many levels, particularly given Google's reliance on YouTube plays for search engine results.

Yet, according to video pro Katie Covell of corporate video production house Sunnyland Pictures, many entrepreneurs undermine their video efforts when they post on YouTube, but fail to follow up by examining that video's statistics. Pretty simple analysis of these markers can reveal primo information, such as:

- **Viewer Demographics.** Demo stats indicate who's watching, making it easy to assess whether or not you're reaching your target audience. For example, Covell pointed to a ladies intimate apparel client whose stats showed younger males watching their videos in droves—not the stylish women 18 to 45 that they wished to reach.

- **Total View Time.** Do people stick around and watch your entire two-minute video? Or do they bail at the 10-second mark? Knowing the answers to these questions can help you consider whether your video is effectively capturing the attention of your audience.

- **Video Scrolling.** Similarly, video scrolling statistics show whether viewers stopped watching and began speeding through your video with the scroll bar. When did they stop watching? And what were they hoping to find?

- **Total Shares/Reposts.** Shares and repost stats are some of the most valuable intel you can gather. Why? Because they indicate that your video has made a significant enough impact for someone to forward on. Did they love your upcoming collection preview? Strongly agree with your nonprofit's underlying philosophical message? Find your new commercial hysterical? Whatever the case may be, shares/reposts show that your business has hit a nerve.

Video Stat Analysis Allows You to Tweak Accordingly

As you can see, even a cursory review of your video stats can reveal so, so much once you know what you're looking for. From there, you can consider tweaks that help you optimize your overall video marketing plan.

Katie Covell has firsthand insight into how even small changes in your video production and related inbound marketing efforts can significantly shift your stats toward your desired business goals. She suggests some of the following troubleshooting tips.

Video Viewing Problem	Potential Solution
Video appeals to wrong demographic instead of target market.	Revise the tone and/or content of the video. Increase inbound marketing efforts (from blog coverage and social media) to get that video in front of your target market.
Viewers stop viewing only a few seconds in.	Make sure your message is immediately clear, and figure out how to hook viewers through humor, how to, and/or heart.
Viewers begin scrolling almost immediately.	Figure out what viewers are looking for and revise video to present that front and center.
No one ever watches my four-minute video all the way through.	For a single-message video, edit your video down to less than two minutes. For multiple messages, edit your video into separate clips.

Chapter 5

Change Your Online Marketing

Standing to Deliver

In my office, I have a framed saying that author and marketing thought leader Seth Godin signed for me. Among other gems, it reminds me that "Oprah has left the building."[1] Seth blatantly tells us to get out of our own way and simply get out there by "picking yourself." Do not wait to be chosen by television folks, interviewers, or the media. You've already thought through what makes you unique (and different enough), why they should choose you, and what kind of value proposition you bring to the table.

Now, how do you stand out online, in a connected land, where there are more blogs than people? (Yes, there are literally more blogs in the United States than the adult population of the United States.) It all starts with understanding (at a particular moment) of your strengths and an ability to communicate those strengths from a home base (your website) in some form of promotion.

Then, it moves to one simple question: How can I genuinely help someone else?

- Are you speaking the language of the people who would be most helped by your products or services?
- Can you explain how they would be helped?
- Have you given them a way to share their experiences and made it easy to spread the word?
- Have you created a community—a place of help?

It may seem like I'm saying that the name of the game is online customer service. *Au contraire!* It's innovation in online mass customization. What does that mean? People want help on their terms, with the exact product or service that might be right for them. They no longer want to settle. There's something to be said for offering both help and choice—and if you can be the one to provide those things, consumers will respond in kind.

Microtargeting is a critical marketing mindset, especially when it comes to the "shop local" movement. Think how you will:

1. Reach and/or attract the people online who will be most helped by your offerings.

2. Explain how you can ease their troubles.

3. Encourage them to become brand ambassadors, who will essentially do your marketing for you.

Tip 21 Ensure That Your E-mail Marketing Is Deliverable

Your first and best marketing resource for microtargeted leads should be your own e-mail database. After all, it contains only people who have visited your website and affirmatively signed up for e-mail updates. You can't get much more micro than that! Your current customers and leads that have sought you ought make up your most fertile future sales demographic; don't make the massive mistake of ignoring this precious resource.

There are entire books written about e-mail marketing—and you should probably buy one of them to continue making progress. For our purposes, however, it is enough to say three things:

• E-mail is not dead. In fact, it's far from it.

• You should sign up with an e-mail service provider (ESP) that increases your deliverability.

• Make sure your list of e-mail addresses is as "clean" and up-to-date as it can be.

Preferred Channel for Permission-Based Promotional Messages (By Age Group)

PROMOTIONAL MESSAGES FROM COMPANIES WHOM I HAVE GRANTED PERMISSION TO SEND ME ONGOING INFORMATION

	OVERALL	15-17	18-24	25-34	35-44	45-54	55-64	65 PLUS
Email	77%	66	74	75	81	79	81	79
Direct Mail (letters, Catalogs, postcards)	9%	6	6	6	9	10	14	14
Text Messaging (SMS) on a cell phone	5%	10	5	7	4	6	1	0
Facebook	4%	8	7	3	4	3	1	0
Telephone	2%	0	5	3	2	1	1	2
Twitter	1%	4	1	1	0	0	0	0
Mobile App	1%	2	1	1	0	1	0	0
LinkedIn	0%	0	0	1	1	0	0	0

Source: Exact Target

E-mail Is Alive and Kicking

According to Forrester Research, corporate America's e-mail marketing spending has been growing 10 percent, year over year. Why? Well, despite users' protests about their overflowing in-boxes, e-mail marketing is still one of the lowest-cost forms of lead generation out there. For every $1 spent, the average return is $44.25 (says Experian). Thus, it should still be a major tool in your sales toolbox.

Don't believe me? Consider that, in 2013, a whopping 44 percent of e-mail recipients made at least one purchase based on a promotional e-mail, according to Convince & Convert's Jay Baer. So, there you go.

If You're Going to Bother Sending It, Bother Getting It Delivered, Too

According to Litmus, 82 percent of people who opt in to your corporate e-mails, actually read them. That is, of course, *if* they receive them.

We kind of take for granted the idea that if we send something, it will be received. In e-mail marketing land, that just isn't so. For example, did you know that Google publicly limits the total number of addresses in the TO, CC, and BCC fields to 99? Therefore, in many cases, even sending an e-mail to 20 people could trigger a filter that would stop the e-mail at the pearly gates of the receiver's mail server—way before the spam filter. End result: no delivery.

There are actual humans working at e-mail service providers (such as Constant Contact, Infusionsoft, MailChimp, and CheetahMail) whose sole role is to work with the major e-mail providers (like Gmail) to make sure their servers are not blacklisted, so that their e-mails actually get delivered. Most small businesses don't have those kind of human resources, though. And, so, SMBs typically hire an e-mail service provider (ESP) to do the dirty work for them.

In fact, deliverability is often the main thing you're paying for when it comes to e-mail marketing. One major ESP, Infusionsoft, has taken pride in raising their deliverability from 90 percent to 99 percent in recent years. How? By lowering their complaint rate statistics, preventing bounces, and eliminating dead e-mail addresses.

James Thompson, Infusionsoft's E-mail Systems Manager, noted, "AOL, Yahoo!, MSN, and those types of companies want to see average complaint rates of about 0.1 percent." According to Thompson, that means that "for every 1,000 e-mails we send, they only want to see one person complaining." [2]

Keep It Clean

It should go without saying that the integrity of your list is just as important (if not more so) than the list's size. Regular "cleaning" of your list (i.e., asking folks to confirm they want to get your e-mails and removing the bounces) leads to higher conversion rates overall. If nothing else, a "clean" list simply costs less to operate. ESPs charge you based on the number of e-mails you have in the database, regardless of how many of those addresses are inactive, bouncing, etc.

Doing It Right

At this point, you may be thinking, "That's great and all, but what about the creative, the messaging, and the calls to action?" Ultimately, those things are of little importance if your e-mail's ending up in the Bermuda Triangle. Start by choosing a solid ESP and only *then* get working on beautiful and carefully crafted messages that sell.

Tip 22 Create Brand Ambassadors

Continue your microtargeting effort by building a contingent of super fans, otherwise known as brand ambassadors. For this effort, elevate a selection of existing top-tier customers to insider status to reap a word-of-mouth windfall. But also think outside of your current contacts and recruit the same zealous support from online thought leaders that fit within your target market.

Though the term "brand ambassador" may be a relatively new buzzword to many, it's certainly not a new concept. I think all of us have been brand ambassadors at one point or another:

> **Brand Ambassador**
>
> Typically, this regular, every-day customer generates buzz—and, to that end, influences other shoppers' buying decisions—by promoting the products or services of a company, both online and offline. This spokesperson, of sorts, is likely to have a "look," "feel," or "voice" that is in line with the brand's values.

- "You absolutely must go to my accountant!"
- "Nordstrom took my return and it wasn't even from their store!"
- "Have you tried Reese's peanut butter eggs? They're so much better than the cups!"

A while ago, I had a great conversation with the founder and CEO of Jock Soap, Josh Harrell, who utilized brand ambassadors to get his line off the ground. Why? "We are able to move more quickly with the Ambassadors (as opposed to other advertising channels)." His advice for building a formidable "embassy"? Harrell urges companies to "start small and make sure your members have a direct line to your marketing team."

Remember, though, that true brand ambassadors are not employees or fan-boys. "They're not fanatics," explained Harrell. "They are generous *friends* of the brand, who truly want to help—and they should be held in high regard."

Ultimately, brand ambassadors are representative of who your target market identifies with. So, what if you made shorts targeted to young men? Well, naturally, you'd love for the big man on campus to talk them up while wearing them. Enter "Chubbies"—men's shorts, with a 5.5" inseam, that harken back to Tom Selleck.

As of this writing, the company has a mere 27 employees at its San Francisco headquarters, but more than 125 "Campus Ambassadors" that represent the brand on college campuses. BuzzFeed wrote, "The company received over 1,000 applications for its campus ambassador program, where Chubbies gives free products to college kids it sees fit to represent the brand on their college campuses ('no jerks')."[3]

ChubbiesShorts.com

As you start "collecting" your own brand ambassadors, ask yourself:

- What would your brand ambassador application look like?
- What would you want your representative to embody?
- Where do these social creatures hang already?
- What do you have to offer them to make them fall in love with your brand?

Tip 23 Understand Search Engine Marketing (SEM) or Find Someone Who Does

So far, we've discussed micromarketing strategies that leverage your existing e-mail database and invite loyal customers and online influencers to sing your praises on high. Now, we'll look at expanding once more, using target market and geographical attributes to get on the radar of the specific categories of people you wish to woo. Let's take a moment to realistically define how search engines, and their reach in display ad inventory on websites, or *their* markets, can actually benefit your specific business without breaking your budget.

Back in the day, you used to be able to find stuff on the Internet. No matter how bizarre or obscure, search engines used to produce answers and results like magic. Now, not so much. Why? Because of various schemes to prioritize the information you receive, all of which have to do with—you guessed it—*money*. Just as with primetime TV ads, there's major value in prominent placement on heavily trafficked search engines. And that's what Search Engine Marketing (SEM) revolves around: getting your company into rotation among search results as paid text, banner, mobile, or video ads. (See ChunkofChange.com/bookgoodies for a detailed diagram showing how the same retailer shows up in a text ad on YouTube, Adwords ad, mobile ad, video ad, and banner ad.)

In addition, Google and their partners, like DoubleClick, have expanded their inventory of ad placement beyond search results, into the content/display network (which takes into account more than 2 million websites that reach more than 90 percent of Internet users worldwide, and approximately three-quarters of the U.S. online audience).

The Minimum to Get Started

The minimum two requirements when starting down the online advertising brick road are:

1. Understanding your customers' interests and/or how they might search for a product or service like yours.

2. Developing a measurable place on your website (ideally landing pages) that take into account what happens after the click.

Cost-Effective Online Efforts

The system of Google's consolidated ad inventory presents major challenges to small business owners, who have to fight to be seen by elbowing in next to large corporations with a lot more *moolah*. At first, the outlook seems grim because of the seemingly insurmountable cost of participation. According to SEM consultant Michele Webb, you'd be looking at an investment of at least $1,500 in advertising spent per month to garner any meaningful return on SEM efforts—a price tag that exceeds many entrepreneurs' entire monthly budget.

So, what can you learn from this? That, in general, custom SEM is cost-prohibitive for most small business owners. But, in a way, that simplifies matters by pointing us toward the very cost-effective, basic building blocks of SEM:

- Search engine optimized (SEO) content that attracts.
- Social media presence that drives (see Chapter 8).

- Turnkey SEM vendor services (such as Google AdWords, Bing Ads, and Baidu).

SEM specialist Michele Webb recommends looking into services offered by ReachLocal.com, which provides personal guidance through their comprehensive range of online advertising tools, such as search advertising and integration of live chat on your website.

Small Businesses' SEM Start: AdWords Strategies

Anyone can use ad networks such as Google AdWords. But not everyone can derive benefit from this type of advertising in the form of viable customer leads. Small businesses especially must employ smart strategies to garner leads while staying on budget.

I spoke to SMB online advertising guru Mark Chapman to find out some best practices for smaller enterprises. One important point that he stressed was the necessity of *patience* in the process of testing and learning. It may seem counterintuitive in the instantaneous world of the Internet, but patience seems key in executing a conservative process of AdWords trial and error.

Key In on Keywords

In an AdWords system, you choose the Internet searchers you want routed to your website by way of keywords. But when it comes to setting up those keywords, less is more. Casting too wide a net with many keyword configurations will get lots of clicks—but you'll pay for each one of them irrespective of the quality of that lead.

Chapman suggests narrowing your keywords down considerably, then testing these selections out one by one over a period of months. This lets you see which terms pull in the best leads without paying out the wazoo for untested incoming clicks. Some ways to accomplish this include:

- **Use keywords that emphasize your unique services**. One of Chapman's clients has tourist accommodations near Disneyland in Anaheim, California. This includes hotel rooms, tent space, and an RV park. The client's initial $300-per-month budget could have easily been wasted by fighting for search engine visibility against the more moneyed, big-name corporate hotels clumped around the Happiest Place on Earth. So instead of "hotel near Disneyland" keywords, Chapman steered the client toward highlighting their other, more unique offerings. After some controlled experiments, they found a winning formula with keywords touting the available RV space, aimed at audiences in the states surrounding California. With a relatively modest monthly investment—and smart strategic advice— the client's online reservations have increased significantly.

- **Use keywords that identify special attributes of your target market**. When designing keyword selections, think of your target market in terms of who, what, where, and when. Who exactly do you expect to walk into your store or buy your product? What will they be looking for and thus plug into a search engine? Where do they live geographically? And when does demand peak for particular services you offer? Instead of simply "best soy candles" you might try "vegan pure soy candles Los Angeles gift." Think longtail (see Tip 15).

Online Ad Network Tips From
Mark Chapman of Everett Andrew Marketing

- Be patient and start small. Try out limited keyword selections over the course of several months. This helps stay within budget while testing what really works.

- Ditch display networks. Table display networks until you have more ad network experience.

- Keep immediacy in mind. Remember that people use search engines to find specific things they know about and want *now*. So don't use keywords focused on new, novel items that have yet to hit public consciousness.

- Avoid AdWords Express. Though many of Google's services simplify the AdWords process for novices, keep in mind that the default settings and suggestions inure to Google's benefit. You know your business best and should carefully tailor your AdWords experience, not just follow Google's cookie-cutter suggestions.

Tip 24 Develop Links Through Inbound Marketing

Keyword efforts help you zero in on precise market segments. But it's your inbound marketing efforts that drive you to the top of search engine results, garnering better visibility to those micromarkets and higher lead volume. With that in mind, let's play a little word association game.

I say, "Inbound marketing."

You say?

[*Crickets.*]

Don't panic. Whether you know the term or not, I'm willing to bet you know a lot more about the subject than you realize. (Kind of like when you bust out into the familiar chorus of that song you swore you'd never heard.)

First Things First: Outbound Marketing Defined

Let's start with outbound marketing, because I'm laying bets that you're definitely aware of these more traditional forms of brand promotion.

- Paid advertisements (television, radio, print, etc.).
- Flyers and direct-mail circulars.
- Spam e-mail.
- Telemarketing (everyone's dinnertime favorite!).

Outbound marketing methods overtly seek to engage the customer in a sales transaction through a direct, open sales pitch. This works extremely well for some products and services (*As Seen on TV* inventions, anyone?), although many will argue that it is dying. For others—well, let's just say there's a reason someone invented Caller ID.

And Now for the Main Event: Inbound Marketing

Inbound marketing, on the other hand, takes a completely different approach—by starting a relationship. Instead of knocking folks over the head with an unwanted sales pitch all caveman-style, inbound marketing seeks to earn customer interest, trust, and patronage by offering something of value, such as useful information or enjoyable online interaction.

Like traditional advertising, inbound marketing has many formats, including:

- Original blog content or contributions.
- Topical e-mails and/or e-newsletters.
- Social media marketing interactions (think Facebook, Twitter, Instagram, and Tumblr).
- YouTube videos, video tutorials, or vlog posts.
- Informative e-books and how-to guides.
- Audio podcasts.

Through these informational vehicles, brands look to earn the opportunity to engage potential customers in an ongoing dialogue. Moreover, these efforts act as digital link outposts that bring people back to the main hub of the business

Link Marketing to Sales to Sharing

cultivate brand ambasssadors that engage, comment, share and attract others to you

BUILDING AN
1 **AUDIENCE**

GETTING NOTICED

feeding the beast, social conversations, search and broadcast

4
ENTHUSIASTIC SHARING

3
CLOSING BUYERS

5
CUSTOMER RETENTION

2
MEASURING CONVERSION

monitor bottom line lag measures, ID relationship to KPIs (Key Performance Indicators)

follow-up with outbound relationship development that encourages forward progress

identify external actions that show interest, develop dashboard with lead measures

look at retention % and lifetime value, use customer relationship management (CRM) technologies

Customize Your Chain at http://bit.ly/olgasMSS

The ideal path takes a new customer from perfect stranger to fanatical brand ambassador. The turns in the path sometimes double back on themselves, like when customers become enthusiastic in their sharing and point new customers to you via social links or good old fashion referral.

It's extremely important to look at the largest part of the Marketing to Sales to Sharing Cycle, the "Getting Noticed and Building an Audience" step along generational lines. Younger generations do not take kindly to anything that whiffs of overt manipulation and broadcast. Instead, content that entertains or informs, and the holy grail of user-generated content (UCG comes in all forms from contributed photos and comments to a yelp review), should be conscientiously cultivated and measured. The hunger for your content contributions is so intense that I call creating engaging content "feeding the beast." Try not to get eaten! Inbound links to your website, article views, comments, overall number of video views, and video view times are just some of the lead measurements that a business may look at up-front.

Conversion, or tracking how many people took an action that shows interest, is its own step. Because different types of businesses will focus on different indicators, key to the equation is placing inbound marketing actions in context according to how they contribute to your ultimate sales goals. Measurement goes hand in hand in each step of the chain.

Money shows itself with closing the buyers in step 3. Yet by focusing solely on sales, you're living in the past, hence the term "lag measure" (coined in the excellent book *The 4 Disciplines of Execution*). Once you see last month's revenue, there's nothing you can do about that number. Therefore, it is important to go up the chain and see what influenceable lead measures can move the needle. Even when we get past the sale, we want to continue to delight the customer so that they will either buy from us again (convert 'em again!) or let others know.

See more detail and customize your own links in the chain at *http://bit. ly/olgasMMS*.

Out-of-the-Box Inbound Efforts

These new "laws of attraction" have come to serve many different roles in business, such as acting as a real-time gauge on who's hot and who's not to the point of dictating how often a fashion model gets booked based on her social media magnetism.

They also serve as a separate metric of total audience, as advertisers seemed to finally appreciate with the launch of Jimmy Fallon's iteration of *The Tonight Show*. Though the newly minted host may not pull the same nighttime numbers as his predecessor, Jay Leno, his consistent ability to serve up next-day viral video hits has earned him a huge online audience. Along with more than 11 million Twitter followers, Fallon has increased his reach across mediums and cultivated 24-hour interaction with his various audiences.

Inbound Marketing Has Exponential Potential

Once you begin efforts to create content and/or a higher online profile, the magical Internet fairies sprinkle pixie dust all around and—*poof*! The invisible online hordes will start promoting your brand, namely by linking back to your blog, video, social media site, etc. Think of all those beautiful digital roadways leading right back to your website. These links become valuable digital assets over time that are just as important as, if not more important than, other items on your business's balance sheet. (See Tips 13 and 38.)

Inbound links are so important that they factor heavily in Google's search results algorithm. The more links to your website home base that reputable websites choose to place on their own sites, the more likely your product or service is viewed as reputable itself, and thus Google thinks highly of the earned hyperlinks leading back to your hub.

How to (Intelligently!) Incorporate More Inbound Marketing

Phew! Okay, now that you're all jazzed to get going, where to begin? Oh, dear. Did I detect a minor deflation of your enthusiasm brought on by the overwhelming question of where the heck to get started?

First and foremost, take things one step at a time. Maybe it's Type A over-ambition, maybe it's a bad case of the Joneses, but many small business owners try to jump into too many new communication channels all at once. Given that small enterprises already struggle with their daily juggling act, stick with one new method of inbound attack.

In selecting your weapon of choice, stay focused on two overarching thoughts:

1. What are you trying to accomplish (building brand awareness with new customers, increasing your e-mail database list,

developing credibility through consistent web presence, driving traffic to your online store, etc.)?

2. Which inbound marketing method can you realistically incorporate into your business, in terms of commitment to follow-through?

Because there's just no sense in launching, say, a new social media effort if you have neither the time nor the inclination to truly nurture that forum. And that's perfectly fine; you can try another inbound avenue, but best be honest up front. It's problematic to set consumer expectations for some steady interaction over time, only to leave them hanging, so carefully consider:

- Content needs.
- Daily/weekly/monthly maintenance of new inbound marketing.
- Availability of human resources (time and aptitude).
- Viability of delegating duties to outside vendors.
- Existing systems and tools.
- Necessary tech updates or hardware acquisitions.
- Sales strategy on traffic increase.
- Costs of implementation.

Don't Invite Guests for Dinner Then Forget to Have Food (That Would Be Rude)

Be forewarned: A lot of really successful inbound marketing efforts nonetheless fail to convert into meaningful sales. Your metrics may be off the charts, with lots of newly created content, consistent promotion through social media, and tons of inbound links from myriad sources that all lead back to your sales hub. It doesn't mean much unless your website home base is set up to convert. (See Tips 17 and 18 for a refresher on conversion.)

It's all well and good to put the word out about your business and invite potential customers back to your website. But the whole effort turns into a big, fat *fail* if your guests show up only to find out you did nothing to prepare for their arrival.

When looking at your big picture plan, think like a department store preparing for the holiday season. Yes, they amp up promotional efforts across the board, with lots of outbound marketing ads, commercials, and circulars, as well as inbound efforts from e-mails, social media outreach, and lots of gift guide recommendations on blogs. But they also pump up their websites with custom content and calls to action, and on the brick and mortar side, hire more sales staff, trick out the store décor, increase signage to point customers in the right directions, and maximize stock—all to make sure they are ready to deliver a seamless sales experience that entices shoppers to buy, buy, buy.

Tip 25 Make Your Video Go Viral!

Now that you've gone through such pains to identify your online micromarkets, you might as well make the extra effort to communicate through their preferred medium: moving pictures. This is the digital age, after all, so go all in with an array of video content.

Chances are, your smartphone takes HD-quality video. So, all you have to do is take some handheld shots of your sweater-wearing cat endorsing your company and wait for the views to rack up, right? Not so fast! Here are a few things you may want to consider first.

Prepping

It's critical that you understand the story that you are trying to tell through your video before you begin. This is where scripting can be vital, to help you concretely think through what you want to say ahead of time. Ask yourself, "Why should people watch this *right now*?" Think specifically. And don't move forward until you have a very compelling answer to that *why*.

Remember the basic reasons that people watch videos (as previously noted in Chapter 4's "Do This, Not That"). In fact, think of the last few videos you watched online. What made you bother to watch them? In all likelihood, they fell in one of these three categories:

- Funny.
- Informational.
- Personally meaningful.

Your video should make it clear to the viewer—*within the first few seconds*—that it will hit one of these buttons. Assume your viewer has a short digital attention span and make sure to get to the point ASAP.

Though you might want to put the long version of your business story on the About Us page of your website, that's not the attention grabbing viral marketing I'm talking about here. When using online video for branding and marketing, just remember that it isn't the medium for miniseries-length messages. Know your point, and get to it before your viewer gets bored.

Planning

When I say planning, I mean putting the video into business context. What's the point of your video in terms of where you want it to lead your audience? To an e-mail sign up? To a product purchase? To simply invite them in to stay a while?

This is the difference between using video to get attention and using video to improve your business. This is how many, many YouTube "stars" have failed to capitalize on their viral video 15 minutes of fame or parlay it into broader success.

To leverage your video to your business advantage, it's imperative that you have a call to action, telling the viewer what they should do next—and, of course, have your analytics ready to record those stats.

Shooting

Once you're ready to film, take pains with presentation. This encompasses both personality and visual aesthetics. Who will the video feature? Is that person (probably *you*) comfortable on camera? And are they ready to engage the viewer with enthusiasm and energy?

Pro Videographer Tip: Image Is Everything!

An online video may be someone's first (if not only) impression of you and your business. So, make sure the quality reflects the professional image you seek to project. It doesn't matter that a surfing instructor may have a wildly different business persona than a lawyer. Just ensure that your videos consistently capture the appropriate tone for your particular industry and clientele.

Setting the right narrative tone depends on the type of video you're crafting, according to video pro Katie Covell. If you're going for:

- **Funny or Fun**. Upbeat and full of crazy, almost weirdly over-the-top energy may fit just right for a funny video or a more lighthearted industry (think kids, entertainment, sports, gaming). If you aim for an entertaining piece, consider having someone in the room with you, just off to the right of the camera. Perform directly to that person and channel the energy of that silent interaction.

- **Informational or Meaningful**. On the other hand, a different approach may be in order for informational and more introspective video pieces. When delivering info, viewers respond to direct communication. Conjure up an image of your target viewer, the type of customer or client you want to attract. Then address the camera directly, as if you're truly speaking to that imaginary individual.

  The same goes for meaningful and thought-provoking pieces, which people find more sincere and authentic with direct communication. In fact, when storyboarding a meaningful video, carefully consider how much to focus on an individual narrator versus visual elements to get your message across.

  As they say, practice makes perfect. Before filming yourself, get comfortable with the way you look on camera using your built-in laptop cam or even a teleconferencing tool like FaceTime. Even if only to capture the mundane (a grocery shopping list, say), logging on-camera minutes will make you feel more natural when it counts.

Recording

Whether you're going for a super slick look or shaky hand-cam style, your sound must be impeccable. Keep in mind: video production can be amateurish and still be wildly popular. In fact, it could be argued that folks like the "authenticity" of keeping it real. But if the sound is too low, garbled, or overshadowed by background noise, viewers will click away in a heartbeat. This completely negates any potential marketing value your video could have had.

In fact, sound quality amounts to such a vital issue that I decided to discuss it at length in this chapter's "Do This, Not That" section. Luckily, there are very accessible (read: inexpensive) solutions available that can produce professional-level sound quality on the most modest iPhone informational video.

Cutting and Editing

Videos should be short and sweet, coming in at less than two minutes. Though that doesn't seem like much time, prepare to edit down a wheelbarrow of raw video in order to get that "simple" two minutes.

Once you've pared your material down, consider how you can add visual interest, which will help hold your viewer's attention. Count how many quick-cuts the last television promo you watched has. Edit in some different angles, cut away to graphics that help tell the story, or just add some fun in there. Check out my blog, ChunkofChange.com, to get some ideas for how to use graphics to help tell your story. (Just don't make it look like that crazy PowerPoint you created when you first discovered transition effects!)

Here are some more pointers:

1. Naming. Where's the shock and awe? Up the ante on your video by understanding that a compelling (or, even better, controversial) title and description are what initially piques someone's interest on YouTube.

2. Disseminating. Have a blogger outreach plan before you release your video. The "Girl learns to dance in a year" booty shaker success was no mistake. Miss Thang had an entire outreach plan that started with e-mails to dozens of bloggers and even to the social outposts of the products in her video.

3. Letting go. Remember that "success" may not mean a million views. Rather, it may mean becoming a steady inbound link to your product page or an easy-to-embed video on a friendly blog.

There's simply no denying the power of viral video. President Obama, himself a master of multi-layered marketing, just had a White House summit of sorts with a handful of bona fide YouTube stars, seeking their assistance as "digital influencers" to tout the benefits of the Affordable Care Act to their online audiences.

What The Research Says With Dr. Norah Dunbar

This chapter is all about using online marketing to reach new customers, but even nonprofit organizations can learn from these ideas.

A recent study by Waters and Jones in the *Journal of Nonprofit & Public Sector Marketing* examined the YouTube videos of the 100 most viewed official nonprofit organization YouTube channels. Nonprofits are turning to social media, and YouTube in particular, because short videos allow organizations to put a human face on their causes and establish their organizational identities. Plus, they allow for greater exposure than would be seen on their own websites alone (considering YouTube is the fourth most visited website in the United States). In fact, these 100 videos were viewed an average of 872,556 times.

Waters and Jones' analysis suggests that nonprofits are not using the YouTube videos to their fullest potential.

1. Only about half of the organizations mentioned their mission statement in their videos, and only 43 out of 100 highlighted their accomplishments and organizational successes. Don't miss out on the opportunity to toot your own horn.

2. Virtually all of the organizations welcomed viewer comments but only 25 percent actually responded to viewer comments or answered their questions. Immediately after the interested viewers have seen the video is the prime time to encourage them to get involved, answer their questions, or clear up any misperceptions.

3. Only about 10 percent of the organizations used their videos to encourage the public to volunteer or donate money to the group. Because these are your most interested viewers, be sure you use the video platform to really sell your most important messages. Think beyond just information-sharing or entertainment.[4]

Case Study

In the Real World: Chris Brogan and His Thousands of BFFs

Meet Rob Hatch

Rob Hatch serves as president of Owner Media Group Inc. and co-founded OwnerMag.com along with CEO Chris Brogan. Rob is OwnerMag's managing director as well as an in-demand executive coach and speaker.

What happens after you've sent your message spiraling into cyberspace, aimed at nurturing existing client relationships and cultivating new ones? How do you connect these efforts to sales conversion, and how do you maintain and troubleshoot as you move forward?

I recently spoke with OwnerMag.com's Rob Hatch about all of the evolving challenges of online marketing. Rob is the operations end behind best-selling author and speaker Chris Brogan's empire of online informational products.

In 2012, the company decided to refocus its efforts. While sending Chris out on speaking engagements (that led to consulting gigs) was a strong income channel, they wanted to refine and expand the ways they delivered information to their clientele. This resulted in consolidating content, taking much of what Chris shared in his speaking engagements, and using that information to create webinars and other informational products intended for a broader audience of entrepreneurs.

This evolution reaffirmed the notion that changes you make should be informed by metrics that show whether your business goals are being met, what actions customers seem to respond to most, and how well your technology tools serve your needs, among other things.

Though they had a website with all the standard bells and whistles, they wanted to maximize its sales potential. They also decided to overhaul their existing inbound marketing e-mail processes in order to:

- Grow their e-mail subscriber network.

- Systematically send out thousands upon thousands of customized e-mails.

- Track key analytics as subscribers clicked through those e-mails.

- Formulate a follow-up strategy that automatically adapted to those analytics.

Result: Within one year of implementation, their revenue stream from online sales grew from approximately 5 percent to more than 40 percent of their overall income. Pretty darn impressive shift.

InfusionSoft: The Right Tool for the Task at Hand

This didn't just happen by accident, but resulted from a lot of deliberation, followed by strategic implementation. After really assessing the functionality needed, the company decided to utilize an e-mail software product called InfusionSoft to map out exactly how they want to communicate with their customers.

Through InfusionSoft, OwnerMag.com delivers a welcome e-mail within a few minutes of new newsletter sign-up, which aims to set the tone for the company's interaction with that person. Hatch noted that this welcome e-mail explains what the company does, gives the recipient the heads up on what to expect in terms of frequency and content of newsletters, and also says up-front that, yes, the reader may be asked to buy from time to time. By not pulling punches and staying true to their stated goals, OwnerMag.com builds credibility while communicating that the ultimate aim is to earn the subscriber's business.

Leveling Up: Creating Value by Delivering Insider Info to E-mail Subscribers

The cornerstone of OwnerMag's e-mail efforts comes in the form of e-newsletters, through which they seek to deliver an authentically personal message

along with top-notch, members-only content that subscribers look forward to receiving.

"An inbox is a really valuable place and takes up real estate," Hatch acknowledges, which is a major reason that OwnerMag.com saves their very best content for their e-mail newsletters, giving subscribers exclusive information that can't be accessed anywhere else.

Both substance and tone factor into the success of their newsletters. And this is where Chris Brogan's communication talents really shine. Despite readers' understanding that a newsletter is, by its nature, meant for a general audience, Chris crafts each e-mail as though he is addressing a single person, capturing a personalized voice that really jumps out at recipients.

Automation Should Increase Interaction Opportunities, Not the Other Way Around

So riddle me this, Batman: Isn't this kind of mass e-mail communication still just a generic replacement for human interaction? Definitely not, according to Rob Hatch, at least not at OwnerMag.com.

To Rob, this kind of automation simply serves as a first step in opening the door to real customer connection. Yes, perhaps the same e-mail goes out to a large number of individuals. But the difference derives from what happens *after* those e-mails go out, when customers actually respond. The value of mass communication comes from telling many people your door is open to them in one fell swoop, leaving time to be directly available for interaction with the few that take you up on that offer.

Hatch lists his direct work e-mail address and an invitation for customer feedback on every outgoing message. This ensures customer responses don't get misrouted or overlooked. Hatch also responds right away to every e-mail that comes in, which he assures is not nearly as onerous as it might seem. Only a handful of responses come back after mass outreach, and even a quick reply to touch base makes a huge impact on the customer's view of their brand. Hatch likens this to the natural interaction a brick-and-mortar store owner would have with a customer who said hello or asked a question: "I would never turn them away."

By supercharging their e-mail marketing and integrating those efforts into a carefully considered sales plan, Owner Media Inc. provides a dynamic, ever-evolving example of how to successfully shift online efforts.

So, you've decided to take the bull by the horns and dive into online marketing with video and sound recordings. Fantastic. Just remember, when it comes to video, sound is paramount. As I mentioned earlier, an amateur video is absolutely fine. You've likely got a serious amount of visual firepower in your cell phone, so producing quality images should be a cinch.

Oddly enough, however, given your cell phone's original function to transmit voice, the quality of its recorded sound leaves much to be desired. It would be a darn shame to take the time and effort to create cool video content only to be stymied by bad audio. Thankfully, simple, inexpensive, kick-butt solutions are available.

Do: Use a nifty external microphone *with* your cell phone, computer, or tablet to create beautiful videos with equally awesome sound quality.

Don't: Use your built-in microphone on your cell phone, computer, or tablet to capture audio for your promotional materials.

Don't you love living in a time where pretty much any conceivable gizmo is just a Google search away? Such is the case with external microphone solutions for every amateur video scenario. By just plugging one of these babies into your video-recording device (again, likely a cell phone, tablet, or computer), you can capture high-quality audio instead of having to settle for the otherwise *meh* quality sound produced by the internal microphone. What good is the strongest marketing message, after all, if it comes out completely unintelligible?

Options really boil down to sound quality, bells and whistles, and price. For example, the plug-and-play iRig Mic Cast ($40 or less), which works with both iOS and Android devices, offers two nice features: a Lo/Hi switch to capture sound at different distances and the ability to hear what you're recording through the headphone jack.

Meanwhile, Zoom just made happy campers of iPhone users the world over with the recent release of its iQ5 external microphone ($100). Although this baby's more expensive, she also comes with a host of additional features that can be used in conjunction with the company's own app or any other native iOS app. We're talking multiple recording file options (WAV, ACC, or RAW), tone control, file splicing—basically more firepower than an advanced novice can handle, but ideal for a technophile, or at least a small business owner with a techie teenager.

Technology changes every day, so I hesitate to get overly specific with too many recommendations. Plenty of solid advice is but a few clicks of a mouse away once you find yourself on the hunt for an external microphone.

Chapter 6

Change Your Sales

How E-commerce Gobbled Up Sales

Selling online shines a light on all of your processes, including your efforts selling offline. According to one report, "70 percent of today's fastest-growing retailers say their e-commerce platforms will become their base technology for digital sales across desktop, mobile, and stores. Most retailers plan to use platforms for in-store payments and mobile commerce."[1]

When most people think about e-commerce, they visualize a web-based storefront, selling products online. It's all about a "buy" button, a shopping cart, and a checkout process. I tend to think of e-commerce a little differently, though. To me, it's really about what your company's online presence, overall, is doing to profit your business.

The modern e-commerce platform is not just about payment for goods sold online. True e-commerce is a much more comprehensive concept now, integrating all aspects of customer experience as essential to marketing, sales, and service. Now, e-commerce begins with attraction. Then the parties can begin to develop trust. The exchange of money for goods and/or services comes last, and only after that foundation of trust has been firmly established. The time from attention to trust to sale can take place in a blink of a mouse-click, or over multiple visits.

E-Commerce Evolution: The Integration of Marketing and Selling

As (oh-so-reliable) Wikipedia points out, the term e-commerce "may refer to more than just buying and selling products online" because it also includes "the entire online process of developing, marketing, selling, delivering, servicing, and paying for products and services."[2] Modern, 24/7, always-on social interconnectedness creates a huge blur and consolidation

E-Commerce as a Mindset

The main point of this chapter is to open up your viewpoint about e-commerce. Modern e-commerce is *not* a one-dimensional equation: ~~E-commerce = Money for Goods.~~

Give e-commerce some credit. It's much more multidimensional than that!

E-commerce = All of your on-line activities that contribute to your ultimate business goal(s)

among selling, marketing, customer service, and technology.

E-Commerce Is All Grown Up

At one time, e-commerce was as simple as using eBay or having a Yahoo store. As things evolve in business, however, they also increase in sophistication. Though those outlets still exist (and continue to thrive), there has been a maturation of the Internet since then. Today, online experiences range in complexity—from giant e-tailers (like Amazon) to home-based crafters (on sites like Etsy).

I'll distill sales through an e-commerce lens for you through the next five tips, and you'll see how strategically thinking through a potential buyer's online experience clarifies the entire cycle.

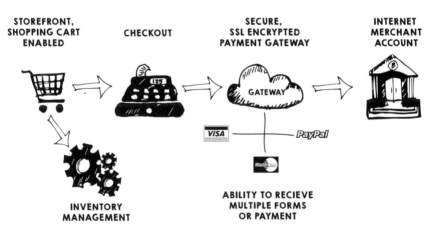

If you want to sell products online, there are a multitude of third-party vendors you can use (or you can create your own solution). Many companies choose a set e-commerce hosting package (from the likes of Square, GoDaddy, Yahoo, Network Solutions, Big Cartel, Shopify, et al.) and work within that framework. Most function as a software as a service (SaaS), online hosting platforms that allow you to access the entire system from within a web browser. This frees you up from having to maintain the IT infrastructure behind the scenes.

> Even a Webhost's 99 percent "uptime guarantee" means that, in a one-year period, you could be *down* for 87 hours! What if that occurred during Christmas rush? Those lost sales are unrecoverable.

In order to create an online storefront, your e-commerce package may include:

- A web server.
- A secure certificate (or encryption).
- The ability to take payments (or gateway).
- The ability to put payments somewhere (or merchant account).
- A system that ties into where that payment is going (your bank account).

There are some companies that offer only bits and pieces of this process and there are others that provide the whole kit and caboodle (including hosting your website).

When you opt for the latter, everything on your site has to fit within the framework of that provider. Sites with a limited number of items for sale will usually go with the simplest all-inclusive options. For a company selling only 50 products, it doesn't really make sense to use a custom solution—unless there's a lot of growth potential.

The custom solutions (like using open-source Magento) are more expensive (because of the programming requirements) than all-in-one hosting solutions but allow for a lot more flexibility. You can't create a custom platform for less than five figures, and it usually involves anywhere from three to 10 times longer to create. The benefit is that the look, feel, and functionality are totally custom and all the parts are secured by you, including all the behind-the-curtain administrative functions.

Regardless of which tack you decide to take, there are a lot of things to consider. On the back end (e.g., the setup of your site, management of your content, and your internal processes and administrative functions), which the customer never actually sees, you need to think about things like your:

- Estimated amount of traffic.
- Checkout process.
- Ease of content management.
- Ability to turn on/off certain functions.
- Inventory management.
- Fulfillment.
- Reporting.

On the front end (i.e., the look, feel, and functionality that shapes the user's experience), you'll need to consider:

- Mobile experience and functionality first.
- Look and feel.
- Ease of navigation.
- Branding.
- Ease of promoting certain products.
- Form and function.

Yes, there's a lot to think about, and it can be overwhelming. This isn't meant to discourage you, however, from starting or improving an e-commerce website. Quite the contrary, in fact. I would say that there's really no time like the present to make the leap.

Why all the fuss over something that only accounts for 9 percent of total retail sales? Well, the rate of e-commerce growth has been roughly three times that of brick and mortar.

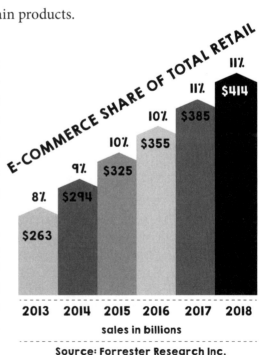

E-COMMERCE SHARE OF TOTAL RETAIL

	8%	9%	10%	10%	11%	11%	11%

$263 $294 $325 $355 $385 $414

2013 2014 2015 2016 2017 2018

sales in billions

Source: Forrester Research Inc.

It's the highest growth channel there is. Furthermore, the functionality of e-commerce makes it so much easier to gather data—which is gold, once actionable—than in a physical store. Ultimately, understanding what that e-commerce data tells you allows you to make more sales over time.

The question isn't "Why should I pursue e-commerce?" but rather, "Why *wouldn't* I want to go after online sales?" Whether you're selling a product or a service, if you have an online presence, you should be thinking about the financial future of your business as it relates to the Internet (and mobile, for that matter).

This chapter may not answer all of your questions about getting started or with optimizing your e-commerce, but it's meant to adjust your mindset—to get you thinking about sales in a different way. To that end, the tips that follow cover:

- How online chat can connect with the friendly, "How may I help you?" vibe.
- Organizing your e-commerce wares by going through the kind of questions I give to clients looking to start an e-commerce site (or dramatically improve an existing one).
- Online loss leaders for service business.
- Looking at how developing trusted content results in more and higher quality sales.
- Tracking sales success and building business systems.

Tip 26 How May I Help You?

Whether you sell widgets or offer professional services, incorporate live chat into your e-commerce life if you have any kind of website, but especially one that has a shopping cart. Online shoppers like online chat. Maybe it's because it's easy. Maybe because it's less frustrating than calling an 800 help line. Maybe it's because people who shop mostly online are actually anti-social and want limited, controlled interaction with other human beings.

But, more than that, I think it's because online shoppers are beginning to shop more like in-store shoppers. They know what they're looking for, and they know, more and more, that retailers are watching their every move online. So they are becoming more comfortable with interacting when approached and expect it when they have questions to ask. It's incumbent on anyone engaged in e-commerce activities to understand this shift and incorporate more personalized service into their online customer experience.

A Case for Live Chat

Live chat offers much more than you may think. It serves to link all of the important aspects of consumer experience: customer questions can be answered, problems fixed, and aggravations soothed. And in serving these needs, your business can close more sales. Additionally, live chat gives critical, real-time feedback about issues that can undermine customer experience (credit card processing down, coupon codes not going through, text on your website doesn't make sense), and thereby cause you to lose business.

Think of live chat like a store employee: on alert for potential in-store problems and available to answer questions and troubleshoot customer issues, but also on hand to facilitate product sales and upsells. It's this multi-functionality, tying together otherwise-disparate aspects of your e-commerce service, that makes live chat not only advisable, but indispensible.

Preaching to the Conversion Choir

Of course, most online sellers want to handle first things first: *How will adding an online chat option increase sales?*

Statistics show much higher conversion rates among live chat users than non-chat users. Live chat gives customers the opportunity to satisfy any lingering concerns and make the purchase jump. When a customer is already primed to purchase, live chat can increase the total tab through strategic upselling. In fact, just as a customer might engage more readily with a friendly in-person sales associate, chatters that respond to a proactive "Hello, let me know if I can help you," are 6.3 times more likely to buy than non-chatters. And, very importantly, a live chat interaction can reveal a wavering customer—a signal that the chat operator may want to direct the sale to another available product or service. Without chat, a wishy-washy customer bounces away; with chat, the sale has been saved.

An Invaluable Tool for Service Providers as Well

Service providers often see e-commerce tools (such as live chat) as only relevant to retailers. But nothing could be further from the truth. Even a solo practitioner can benefit from using live chat services. Live chat makes it possible for even telecommuting professionals to transform their website into a brick and mortar office space, the place where they can be available to greet and address questions from virtual foot traffic.

In this day and age, people want something *now* once they decide they want it. Adding another avenue of availability gives service professionals one more way to set themselves apart from others in their field.

Live Chat Is Super Easy to Incorporate

One of the reasons I advocate adding a chat function is because it's so darn easy nowadays!

My top two options are BoldChat, which gives an easily integrated dashboard that allows users to actively monitor the people browsing in their online store, and Olark, which has all of the basic benefits but costs zero, zilch, nada.

The only way to find out which option will work best for you is to do a little research, scout out useful solutions that have worked for others, and begin trying things out. And be sure to check out this chapter's "Do This, Not That," which offers some additional tips for delivering the best live chat service to your customers.

What the Research Says With Dr. Norah Dunbar

This chapter is all about the different ways that you can use e-commerce tools to your advantage when communicating with customers.

One thing that often happens in a store is that we engage in "impulse" purchases that are not planned before we go. Why else would they put the chocolate bars right next to the checkout in the grocery store? According to a research study led by Yong Liu in the journal *Decision Support Systems*, about 40 percent of the money spent on e-commerce sites is attributed to impulse purchases. A pleasant on-line shopping experience can encourage shoppers to buy.

The study found these variables were most related to impulse purchases:

- The website was easy to navigate.
- The website was visually appealing.
- The website offered an attractive assortment of products.
- The website offered instant gratification because the product seemed immediately available.
- The purchasers had personality traits that led them to impulsiveness. (This is typically found in young users who prefer instant purchases like downloads that are available immediately.)

Tip 27 Realize Your Dream of Passive Income

Many fledgling entrepreneurs harbor dreams of setting up the perfect Internet enterprise, envisioning a totally computerized process, a fully automated channel that doesn't require constant attention. Still others may mistakenly believe that they cannot use the Internet to sell, because they primarily offer services or just want folks to donate to their cause. This tip serves to dispel both views.

First, even if a customer's online shopping and payment experience may be self-service, there's quite a bit of human interaction required behind the scenes to make that sale possible. Just because you're not holding your visitor's hand doesn't mean it's a "hands-free" transaction. And, nothing in the business universe survives (let alone *thrives*) running solely on autopilot. Second, you needn't dismiss Internet sales dreams just because your enterprise is primarily or entirely service based. You simply need to look at how you might commoditize your skills.

Making Your Service a Product

If you are a professional who offers services, you can still sell products online. You simply need to turn your service into a product. You might consider offering:

- Packages for your offline offerings.
- Worksheets/checklists.

- White papers or expert reports for a niche industry.
- E-books.
- Webinars.
- Consulting via chat, Skype/FaceTime, or clarity.fm scheduled calls.
- Service packages.
- Subscriptions to premium content.
- Access to communities (i.e., private Facebook groups).
- Live workshops via "masterminds."

I'm sure there are many, many more formats in which you can present your professional knowledge. But the most important point I'm making here is that you change your mindset and consider how to package your skills into something that can be sold *en masse*.

Integrated Online Product Sales

Selling online is not as simple as the self-executing, self-sustaining pipe dream discussed above. But there are definitely ways to set up a retail endeavor that automates those things that can be automated, leaving precious time and resources for you to think about more important business matters.

In this regard, it's important to properly replicate the "human touch points" that you'd have in a brick-and-mortar operation (e.g., greeting customers, taking inventory off the shelf and re-stocking, etc.). You are not a nameless, faceless, electronic vending machine. Real-world customer service must be translated into online customer experience.

Alas, not all charming in-person experiences translate well to the web. It's precisely why that super-cute Victorian boutique on Main Street doesn't do well online. That store's website doesn't (and perhaps *can't*) adequately replicate the feeling of the offline shopping experience. Without the ambience, shoppers are likely to buy their doilies and tea cups elsewhere—through a site that's easier to use and has lower prices. However, the boutique can use their online presence to drive offline commerce, even if their doilies don't prove hot sellers online.

As in the brick-and-mortar world, in the online arena, you have to decide what your "-est" is. (See Chapter 1 for a full explanation of this concept.) An e-commerce "-est" is something that calls attention to why someone should buy from your website rather than a competitor's (i.e., you're the cheapest or the most trustworthy, you offer the best selection or best shopping experience, or a combination of things).

The Real First Step in Online Sales

Although customer experience is incredibly important, you can't really start there. The first step is properly configuring the items you have for sale. You really have to think about how you want to organize your site, and how you want to sell. For instance, when it comes to your product, do your customers typically shop by style first or by color?

It may seem like a strange question, but the way people shop will determine how you should organize the data on your site. It's so important, that I dedicated an entire tip to this topic alone. After it's set up a certain way, it can be exceedingly difficult to change. So, it's essential to put some thought into this process early on. Unfortunately, a vendor can't answer these types of questions for you. You know your customers—and your market—better than anyone else. Time to create some e-commerce assets. (See Tips 13 and 38 on how to add valuable assets and safeguard them in your digital asset locker.)

Start by creating a simple spreadsheet of your products. The format isn't actually as important as the information. At some point, these details will be translated into the database for your e-commerce solution. The very basics are things like product number, product name, price, short and long description, and weight. Start there and then, as you go through the questions that follow, you'll be able to add additional columns (e.g., product category, variants, etc.) and useful details that will allow a programmer to help you more effectively. I'll help you out at ChunkofChange.com/bookgoodies by providing a simple e-commerce spreadsheet for your use.

Moose Boots, Your Online Source for Dog Booties and Silly Socks, Shows the Way

To illustrate these points, I've created an imaginary business: Moose Boots, a company that makes shoes and socks for dogs. Using this example, I'll go through the questionnaire I use with my clients, offering explanations about each point along the way.

I'm limiting this tip to the specific things that fall into the realm of product "Operations & Logistics," including general and detailed product information, special selling factors, taxes and shipping, and inventory controls. Answering these product questions now will save you from additional cost and heartache as you move toward setting up shop online.

GENERAL PRODUCT INFORMATION

Question	Moose Boots' Answer	Why is it important?
What kinds of products will you be selling?	Socks and shoes for dogs	Not only is it important to be able to succinctly communicate what you are selling, it's important to understand that different types of products have different requirements.
What is the estimated number of products you'll be selling?	6: Hiking boots, rain boots, snow boots, tube socks, no-skid socks, legwarmers	The more items you sell, the more have to be maintained. This question alone may determine how sophisticated your e-commerce solution needs to be.
Will products be sold with multiple variants (such as different sizes or colors)?	Yes: All items are offered in blue, red, or green. All items come in S, M, L, and XL.	The word "variant" really refers to an item's variables (or, the choices a customer has for different versions of the same product). The same item may come in different colors, sizes, or styles.
How many product categories will you have?	2: Shoes, socks	Categories are the stepping-stones of how your online catalog will be organized.

Will it be possible for one product to be associated with multiple categories?	Yes: No-skid socks appear in both the sock and the shoe category.	This is typical online because, ultimately, you want to provide many paths for someone to find the product. (In the offline world, in a grocery store, avocados may be in the produce section and also located next to the chips.)
How many manufacturers will you be working with?	2: Shoe maker, sock maker	The first part of this is that customers might need to be able to search by brand. The second part of it has to do with your inventory maintenance.
Are any of your products digital/downloadable?	No	This may include e-books, music, or other downloads. You may not have to worry about fulfillment or shipping for these kinds of items, but you do have other considerations. How is the information going to be shared? How do you keep it from being pirated? Will you offer a digital key or code?

PRODUCT DETAILS

Question	Moose Boots' Answer	Explanation
Do you already have item numbers or stock keeping units (SKUs) for your products?	Name and color, but not SKUs	You need a unique identifier for each product, as well as all of its variants. Start out with a good scheme with coding that makes sense for your industry.
Do you already have short and long descriptions for each product?	Yes	When a user searches for a product on your site, there will be different types of pages that display those products. Based on the type of page, it may be more appropriate to have a short description than a long one. They may also be useful for coding purposes. A long description makes more sense for an item detail page.

Do you already have photos of each product that will be sold (preferably on a white background)?	Not yet. Need to take lifestyle photography (on models) in addition to product shots.	Create uncomplicated, yet systematic file names and locations, so that photos will be easy to find and access. (For example, the item, the style, and the shot: 3579_Blue_Front.jpg)
Do you already have prices set for each product?	Yes: Wholesale and MSRP. Discounts for aging?	Some manufacturers in the offline world may have different prices for different customers. Online, however, you need to have a set retail price and a set sale price.
Will any of your product's variants affect price?	Yes: Size XL costs an extra $5.	Color did not affect the price, but the size variant did. In this case more raw material lead to a higher manufacturing cost, and Moose Boots requires the higher cost passed on to the customer.

PRODUCT DATABASE

Question	Moose Boots' Answer	Explanation
Is your product information currently stored in a database or Excel/CSV file?	Google Docs Spreadsheet	Even if you don't think you have a "database," a simple Excel file of your product details is useful. On the other hand, Word files (with embedded tables) are nearly impossible to work with.
Will you need to do bulk uploads of product files?	Yes, definitely! Every season there are new styles.	Do you really want to manually input all of your data into the system? Probably not. No matter what software you use, there should be an online tool available that will allow you to export/import data.

SPECIAL SELLING FACTORS

Question	Moose Boots' Answer	Explanation
Will you bundle products together and sell them as one item?	Yes: Rain boots and legwarmers are sold as a Christmas gift set.	Most systems will require the bundle to have a unique item number or will automatically generate one with a differentiator.
Will some specific products only be sold with other specific products?	No	The best example of this is a computer. You start with a basic system, add memory, add sound, add a graphics card, and so on. Often, there are rules associated with this process (e.g., "If you add A and B, you can't add C").
Would you like to be able to cross-sell or up-sell?	Yes: Both	A cross-sell tends to be a "you may also like..." message. An up-sell usually happens at cart level, and appears as "if you purchase one more item, you get $5 off" or "add another $9 worth of items and get free shipping."

TAXES AND SHIPPING

Question	Moose Boots' Answer	Explanation
Have you determined the tax class (if applicable) for your products?	I will only charge tax in my own state.	There are varying local tax requirements for products sold online.
Do you know the weight of each product?	I want to ship everything in a Priority Mail box where size, not weight, determines price.	Shipping options and costs are typically based on an item's weight.

INVENTORY CONTROLS

Question	Moose Boots' Answer	Explanation
How will you keep track of your inventory?	I will physically count inventory once a week and put into the Google Docs spreadsheet, but would like to find an on-line system I can put it into instead.	What has been sold? What will you need to reorder from manufacturers/ vendors?
If you sell out of an item, what will happen on the front end of your site? Will customers still be able to see that item?	I want it to still show. Can I offer as backorder?	If you run out of inventory of a certain product, does that item just stop showing up on your website? If so, it can be really confusing for the customer.

Tip 28 Creating Loss Leaders for Local Service Businesses

Service providers, from lawyers to accountants to hair stylists to plumbers, can all benefit from increasing their e-commerce actions. Yet, many shy away from this, often based on the misperception that e-commerce only relates to selling widgets. Though advice about how to streamline your storefront and integrate your delivery methods may not be wholly on point, there is so much more to e-commerce than that! When looked at instead as a toolbox chock full of many different tools, a sole practitioner is suddenly empowered to use only those tools that help him or her play to pre-existing strengths.

Example: Small Yoga Studio Uses Loss Leader to Gain Long-Term

In an effort to attract new long-term clients, Kava Yoga (kavayoga.com) in Long Beach, California, runs an unbeatable "10 days for $10" special. At first, a sandwich board outside the front door proclaimed this special; later, they utilized the enticement on their first Google AdWords campaign.

As anyone interested in yoga comes to find out pretty darn quick, $10 would be a good price for even a single yoga class here in Southern California. So, the opportunity to thoroughly try out a new studio and get familiar with its schedule and instructors for only 10 bucks pretty much kicks butt.

Suffice it to say, the studio must lose money on such a low-cost proposition. Yet they continue to run this deal for new customers because it has proven successful to their long-term goals of building a solid base of repeat customers that pay full price for classes.

How to Generate Leads With an Irresistible Loss Leader Special

So how can your service business create its own loss leader to bring in leads? First, understand that loss leaders by definition *lose money*. So you need to look at your deal as an investment in hot leads. Even so, a business owner should never offer a killer deal without seriously considering how to derive benefit from that transaction, whether through instant upselling, garnering stellar reviews and/or word of mouth, or developing long-term business relationships.

- Consider the overarching goals you want your loss leader deal to serve.
- Choose a low-cost, high-demand item or service to offer as a special incentive.
- Brainstorm all of the ways to upsell that item or service.
- Market your deal through strategic online and offline channels.
- Deliver excellent service and solicit positive reviews.

Tip 29 Trusted Content Results in More Online Sales

By now, everyone's heard of the Nigerian e-mail scam, right? I'm sure those funds in the troubled Nigerian prince's account will transfer to my checking account any day now. So why won't that pesky phishing scheme just go away? Because Internet thieves follow the P.T. Barnum philosophy that "there's a sucker born every minute." The scam still exists because there are still people to defraud and brand-new unsuspecting victims logging online as soon as their parents put a cell phone in their hands.

How does this affect you, exactly? Through ripple effect. Savvy online shoppers know the dangers of the Internet and proceed with caution. This makes legitimacy and credibility critical to developing the kind of customer trust required to build your business.

Expert Content = Long-Term Credibility

There are many ways to build business rapport. But trusted content is an excellent area to explore, especially for smaller concerns with budget considerations. What might this entail, exactly? Nothing more than playing to your strengths.

Trusted content consists of simply creating in-depth information related to your top products and product lines—not in the way of individual product descriptions, but information that presents more general information, such as:

- An overview of the product segment.
- How-to information on how to select products in that segment.
- Lifestyle information relevant to product users.
- General safety information.
- "Best of" lists.

Early-Bird Special

An old adage says that the early bird gets the worm, and that's true when it comes to trusted content, as well. General information on a product segment helps catch consumer attention very early on, just as they begin to research something of interest. Think of the questions your interested, but very new, customers might ask as they browse through your store.

By positioning yourself as an authority on a topic, and providing truly useful information about that subject, you begin to establish a positive relationship with a potential customer. Now they feel you have provided good, trustworthy service and assistance, just like an excellent customer service associate would at a real-world store. By offering this type of assistance at this early stage, you have the opportunity to proactively capture a customer's attention and walk them through the process, from initial interest through to sales.

REI: Reaping Rewards of Expert Content Efforts

Much time, effort, and money has gone into figuring out how to go out and get customers and leads, including paid leads. Yet many companies are spending more and more resources figuring out how to get hot leads to come to them. Sounds simple, but just as a geographically challenged brick-and-mortar shop may have difficulty catching public attention through marketing efforts, so can an online enterprise with innumerable competitors in the vast endless universe of cyberspace.

Instead of relying solely on traditional e-commerce lead generation techniques, outdoor lifestyle retailer REI has begun to emphasize expert content creation to its sales efforts. REI has added a great deal of informational content to its website that focuses on its top retail segments and the outdoor lifestyle.

Take, for example, one of REI's top categories: paddleboards. You would expect a top retailer to pop up if a person searches for "buy paddleboard" or "where to buy paddleboard." But REI's expert content captures an even broader swath of search results. So guess which retailer a potential customer will see after searching for "how to paddleboard," "choosing a paddleboard," and "is paddleboarding safe?" That's right: REI.

REI uses a tool called Conductor Searchlight to track the success of its expert content campaigns for topics such as paddleboarding and rock climbing. And its success rates have been pretty amazing: A 300-percent higher customer acquisition rate when using the expert content platform compared to control test groups.[3] Moreover, they're seeing a 16-percent-higher conversion rate from customers entering their website through these expert content pages than those entering from traditional e-commerce channels.

Develop Your Own Expert Content

As noted above, developing your own trusted content is a relatively straightforward and cost-effective way to boost your e-commerce efforts. Here's how it works:

1. **Assess your top products/product segments.** Looking at your best-sellers and top product segments gives a good starting point. These will also likely be areas you and your staff are particularly well-informed about, making content creation a relatively simple process.

2. **Create and post related, in-depth, informational content.** Every small business owner has expertise in his or her own business, or can rely on knowledgeable staff members. Cull from that knowledge to create high-quality informational content that anticipates the questions new customers might ask.

3. **Utilize tracking tools to monitor and tweak.** Using content analytics, such as Conductor Searchlight, can help you assess the content you need to catch your customers early on in the sales cycle.

Think of the building of your own expert content much like the building of a very special entrance to your store, one where you have your most knowledgeable and helpful staff on hand simply to answer people's questions about not only your products, but about how to choose them and use them as well. By providing great information in a no-pressure environment, you've stoked consumer trust early on, ensuring you'll be their go-to retailer once they decide to buy.

Tip 30 Tracking Sales Systematically to Success

You can thank Amazon and social e-commerce in general for your customer's expectation of access to you 24/7 in a highly engaging and personalized way.

> "It's about understanding your customer: what channel they're using, what they want to do with you, and then being able to enable those journeys or those conversations and doing it in a way that's personal; not creepy personal, but personal.... We're still in the very early days...but I have [kids] and they live their lives in a very different world than we do. It's very much an online, instant gratification, instant connection type of world."[4]
>
> —Kate Leggett, Forrester Research Analyst

Hopefully, at this point in the book, and especially in this chapter, you have come to see that the lines between sales and marketing have completely blurred when it comes to business in the e-commerce age. Instead, it's best to look at these areas as part of a complementary cycle within your business, like the Marketing to Sales to Share links in Tip 24. Thus, any efforts you can undertake to integrate your efforts in these areas will help improve stats for both sales and marketing in an efficient and scaleable way.

This can begin simply through taking note of your sales successes and tracking that information. Then you can try out some different tools—from a simple spreadsheet to advanced online systems—to bring you some clarity on what's been working, the forward motion of your staff, and where to focus in the future.

The majority of this chapter has focused on some key upgrades, tweaks, and changes you can make to leverage your existing online sales presence. By adopting some of those suggestions, and a new perspective on how all aspects of e-commerce flow together, you can effect major changes in your sales income on a global level.

Once You Understand Your Own Sales Cycle, Automate It

I waited until now to introduce this term, Customer Relationship Management (CRM), because I didn't want to bog down the conversation with terminology that might turn you off. But CRM can really be as simple as Lorenda's suggested follow-up sales spreadsheet. (See box on page 166.) In fact, spreadsheets such as this have been a cornerstone of my own business practices for years.

However, depending on your business and your vision for scaling up, you may seek more technology-based CRM solutions, in the form of "software as a service" (SaaS) that aims to automate part of your sales cycle. Because SaaS has been traditionally viewed as a sales tool, it is often used to develop leads and effectuate sales. Often, however, users neglect to leverage SaaS for follow-up and customer service.

This is where small businesses have the opportunity to shine compared to some of the behemoth corporations. Large, established companies have built their business around static, independent departments. Each department has its own technological system, its own silo of information, if you will. But, as discussed at the top of this chapter, the explosion of CRM technology during the past 20 years (which is still growing at more than 10 percent a year) has fundamentally changed the marketplace; sales and marketing and every other department are now intertwined and truly synergistic in the e-commerce age.

And that's where large corporate entities stumble, like the lumbering dinosaurs that they are, struggling to move quickly despite the lack of internal integration. But you—small, streamlined, agile—*can*. And that is how you can serve your customers better.

Document Your Customer's Journey

How did you land this sale? Take a moment to look inward and document.

Look at your recent history of customers and sales. This is just one more way that e-commerce makes your life easier; most of this information should be readily available within your sales database and reports. What do you know about these people that goes beyond their psycho-graphic profile and dip into their online behavior?

Cull from your recent past; think about the last 10, 50, 100 customers (depending on your business) and look for *patterns*. Who are they? Where are they? Why did they buy? What would the most effective follow-up be?

Lorenda Phillips has worked with more than 3,000 business coaching clients, taking many small business owners to seven-figure revenue and beyond. For every sales transaction there are four phases:

1. Discovery (questions are asked; trust is built).
2. Presentation/Integration (what you learned in the discovery phase).
3. The Ask.
4. Life after (upsells, referrals are examples).

The people who close the most business track all the steps, throughout the process:

- Name.
- E-mail.
- Phone.
- Address.
- Others involved.
- Decision date.
- Notes.

Lorenda notes, "Every time I talk to someone, I note it somewhere and put the next action in my calendar. If there is no action, I put in the dead file. No more is it important to have courage and integrity than in sales: courage because you have to deal with your demons to be intimate and ask for the business; integrity because you have to do what you say throughout the sales process. You break the trust, you lose the sale."

Start with guesses, and then look through your data to back up your guesses or get you a clearer picture of the actual paths that got your customers to choose you.

Blurred Lines: The Sales and Marketing Remix

In my opinion, the two industry leaders for SMB software solutions that take into account the blurred lines of sales and marketing are Salesforce and InfusionSoft. Interestingly enough, one solution (Salesforce) began as a sales tool that has evolved to incorporate marketing needs; the other was designed with a marketing focus (InfusionSoft) that built out the CRM processes from there. I know of many, many business owners, with companies of all shapes and sizes, who have had success with these tools. Both, however, require a significant up-front investment in time and a recurring fee forever.

Start Somewhere—Start Here

If you're totally green in this arena, ease yourself into the fray by first mastering Lorenda's spreadsheet. From there, feel free to get your feet wet by picking a free CRM tool, such as Zoho. (Also worth a look: Batchbook, Pipedrive, Capsule, Highrise, SugarCRM, and Relenta.)

Shortcut Alert! Moving Beyond the Spreadsheet to Full Integration for FREE!

By far my favorite and recommended sales success system integrates two free tools directly within Gmail: Yesware and Rapportive

Yesware.com offers mind-blowing e-mail tracking, scheduling, Google calendar follow-ups, and seamless CRM integration with Salesforce.com's advanced features and all the other CRMs mentioned above, plus Nimble, Netsuite, Nutshell, and TimeTrade.

Rapportive's right panel populates automatically when you receive or are drafting a message and shows the person's picture and direct links to the contact's social networks

Note: This shortcut requires that you use Gmail on the Chrome browser.

One great advantage of trying out and/or adopting a software solution comes from becoming a part of the community of users of that product. Tapping into user forums and events can not only help you troubleshoot the program, but provide a wealth of ideas and insights from other similarly-situated business professionals. By connecting with other folks with similar goals and roadblocks, you can exponentially increase your trial and error knowledge through collective effort.

In the Real World: Rose Park Roasters

Respected craft coffee purveyors Rose Park Roasters wanted to update their clunky WordPress website with an e-commerce system that could take their sales beyond the local coffee houses, bakeries, and restaurants it supplied. They also wanted to clearly differentiate their brand by telling their story of bicycle-delivered fresh roasted coffee on their online home base, RoseParkRoasters.com.

The guys behind the brand, Nathan and Andrew, came to my day job, creative agency ohso! design, with a very limited budget. They thought of e-commerce as simply a way to directly reach coffee connoisseurs and take payments online.

In reality, though, the website's potential was much more than just a payment gateway. By changing to an e-commerce mindset, they had an opportunity to grow their revenue substantially and provide a great new service through a game-changing concept that previously eluded them: automatic coffee subscriptions.

> "The subscription model is great! If your customer service is on point and you have a good product, then you can expect a subscribing customer to be worth 10 to 30 times your product sale price."
>
> —Nathan Tourtelotte, founder of Rose Park Roasters

External e-commerce platforms are notorious for being difficult to customize. That frustration includes customizing the look and feel of the site, the back-end content management, and also any custom options.

In this case, we needed the vendor to not only code the coffee subscription as an item with a recurring billing cycle, but also integrate several variants into the product offering itself. (See the "Moose Boots" example in Tip 27 to understand more about variants.)

We Deliver Weekly, Bi-Weekly, Tri-Weekly and...Every Four Weeks.

As opposed to a bag of beans that has one set of variables, having a subscription required three sets of choices:

1. Selecting the type of coffee in your subscription (Roaster's Selection, Always Espresso, or Always Decaf).
2. Selecting the type of grind.
3. Choosing delivery frequency.

On the back-end, all of these choices tie into the billing system to trigger related e-mail messages and automatic payment. We researched multiple options and settled on external vendor 3dcart.com because of a low monthly fee (less than 500 products is $20/mo), relative ease of use, and options to customize look and feel. ohso! design provided design tweaks to customize the look and feel of the site, as well as consulting in order to integrate the custom subscription code into the overall plan.

"The subscription model is great!" raves Nathan of Rose Park Roasters. "I don't know if we would have any e-commerce business to speak of if it weren't for subscriptions. Subscriptions comprise 80 percent to 90 percent of our online business in any given week, and 85 percent of all the people who have ever signed up are currently still subscribers."

Do: Utilize live chat to directly interact with your customers in a personal, truly service-oriented manner.

Don't: Utilize live chat in a canned, robotic manner that alienates customers.

The differences between the in-store and online shopping experiences are rapidly disappearing. This allows online entrepreneurs a huge opportunity to actively engage with potential clients just as they would in person.

Start thinking about live chat communication through the lens of in-store customer service and sales. The more personal and responsive you make the experience, the more your customers will repay you in goodwill, word of mouth recommendations, reviews, and sales. Be sure to:

- **_Deliver Some CEO Lip Service._** Nothing delivers quite the same customer experience as direct interaction with the proprietor of an establishment. The same is true online. Try manning your own live chat lines! Once your (sometimes-cynical) customers realize you're the CEO, they'll be really excited about receiving customer service from the big cheese.

- **_Embrace the One-Way Mirror._** Even if a customer prefers the relative anonymity of interacting online through live chat, that sentiment only flows one way. No one gets the warm fuzzies from talking to a robot operator. Boost your credibility by providing customers some personal information. I'm not saying you need to disclose your social security number or anything. I'm just suggesting that you offer, at minimum, your name and a picture—and maybe a little profile.

- **_Make Your Operators in Your Own Image._** You can't man the live chat lines 24/7. But you can provide your operators the resources to offer the same level of service that you would yourself. Assess your most common customer questions and concerns, and provide detailed information to your live chat provider. And test the system yourself, engaging in secret shopper–style live chat sessions to assess the quality of the service being delivered.

Chapter 7

Change Your Reviews

Joining the Conversation

Reviews are powerful and only getting more so every day. Not only has the review process become integral to sales, but it's quickly becoming one of the major ways that people search online for businesses.

Typically business reacts to reviews in two ways:

1. Ostrich style. *If I don't see the reviews, they don't exist.*

2. Control-freak style. *I'm gonna manipulate the reviews by gaming the system.*

And here is where the ultimate opportunity presents itself. By becoming part of the conversation that exists with or without you, reviews become a tremendous opportunity to:

- **Get noticed.** The number-one filter for most people looking to make a purchasing decision is whether something has reviews—at all. If your website, your product, or service doesn't have any, that's a sure fire way to not even be in contention.

- **Become a trusted authority.** This can be accomplished when you jump in and help to clarify or provide a feeling of trust with a comment.

- **Connect in an increasingly disconnected world.** People crave connection as a basic human need; by being part of the conversation, you serve that need.

Have Positive/Negative Reviews Influenced Your Buying Decisions?

http://www.zendesk.com/resources/customer-service-benchmark

Everyone's a Critic (No, Really)

Forget what you think you know about reviews. The era of the professional critic is gone. Today, everyone who walks through the door is a critic.

The fact is that reviews have changed dramatically during the past 15 years. The phenomenon really started in 1995 with Amazon.com, which allowed customers to review products. Many other retailers followed suit, broadening the scope of things being reviewed. During the late 1990s, bloggers also began putting their two cents in. In 2003, LinkedIn came on to the scene, enabling people to review their coworkers and peers. Then, Yelp cropped up in 2004 to provide consumers with a way to review the places they frequented and services they used. Although it started as primarily a restaurant review site, Yelp quickly came to accept reviews on just about anything that has an address associated with it.

Of course, these are only a few examples, but the number of sites out there providing a forum for reviews is virtually endless. Now, the span of reviews is even going beyond people, places, and things. The bottom line is that you can no longer *avoid* being reviewed—no matter what your business is. The reviews are already out there. Even if you're not online, your customers are. The goal is to become an active participant in the review process.

The Only Thing to Fear Is Fear Itself

All of that said, don't be afraid of reviews and the review process. There's a real power in being reviewed—and that power is in your favor. Reviews not only give potential customers information about your products or services, they also are proven to:

- Generate new leads.
- Establish trust and credibility.
- Boost same-product sales.
- Increase average order value.
- Decrease returns.

In addition, as search engines crawl the web, your reviews can increase search traffic and, in turn, boost search-related sales.

There are a host of things you can do to get your business noticed online and reviewed by users. The good news is that nearly all of these things are *free*! (I've limited the recommendations here to exclude any sites that have a membership or sign-up fee.) In the five tips that follow, I'll show you how to get listed and how to get reviewed.

Tip 31 Understand the Power of Online Reviews to Your Advantage

In a vast world of choice (see Tip 49), people need a way of bringing order to the madness. When it comes to online shopping, consumer reviews serve that purpose.

You cannot—no! *must* not—bury your head in the sand in an effort to avoid seeing any bad reviews. You have to adjust your thinking and your approach to reviews, seeing just how omnipresent they truly are and looking at them as an opportunity, instead of something to fear. With that in mind, my first tip is to expand your view of reviews: what form they take, where they can be found, and the innate opportunity they present.

In cultivating your reviews, you are helping customers develop a more comprehensive picture of you, your company, and your products. View reviews as one of your biggest assets, as uber-valuable testimonials that give new users confidence in you and lead to new business.

A World of Omnipresent Reviews

Other than everywhere, where, specifically, are you being reviewed? Well, let's take a gander, shall we?

- Shopping destinations (such as Amazon, eBay, and Etsy) if you are a product manufacturer or you use their marketplace as a distributor.
- Local "directories" (such as Yelp, Angie's List).
- Local results on search engines (such as Google Local and Bing).
- Your own website's built-in product reviews or included testimonials.
- Hyper-local community websites (like NextDoor.com), where neighbors ask for recommendations and share their experiences with local vendors.
- In the Social sphere (on LinkedIn, a random tweet on Twitter, or a Facebook wall).
- Specialty-focused websites for your industry.
- Shoot! Even Uber's cabbies now rate you, their fares. (Hey, turnabout is fair play!)

Positive Reviews Earn New Business

People want to go with tried-and-true choices. And they will gladly accept the recommendations of a complete stranger, if they believe the veracity of the stranger as a fellow consumer. Moreover, they hold the collective opinions of many strangers in exponentially higher esteem: not only do they lend credence to the individual opinion, but they look at a consistently well-reviewed item as having universal appeal and utility.

**What the Research Says
With Dr. Norah Dunbar**

Online reviews are an extremely important part of the e-commerce world because buyers rely heavily on the opinions of fellow users and expert reviewers, especially when considering an expensive purchase (like booking a vacation). Before we had online shopping, we had word-of-mouth reputations. Shoppers would ask their family, friends, and neighbors about their experiences with a business or product. As a result, online product reviews are sometimes called eWOM (which stands for electronic word of mouth).

One study, done by Matthew Jensen and colleagues at the University of Oklahoma and published in the *Journal of Management Information Systems*, investigated the perceived credibility of eWOM reviews. This study showed mock reviews of a digital camera and showed them to likely buyers to examine the effect. They found:

1. Most reviews are typically one-sided in that positive reviews only talk about the positive aspects of a product and negative reviews do the opposite. But when they introduced two-sided reviews that discussed both the benefits and deficiencies of a product, the reviews were seen as more credible.

2. Using more complicated language did not make the review sound more credible. Although it might sound fancier to use more technical terms, longer words, and more complex sentences, that had little effect on how credible the review seemed to the shoppers.

3. More emotionally intense language made the review sound *less* credible. Though you might think that passion or intensity would make a reviewer seem committed to their opinion, it also was a turn-off for shoppers. They preferred less emotional reviews when evaluating credibility.

Tip 32 Make Sure Your Business Appears in Local Search Results Correctly

In terms of using reviews as an opportunity, you can't get much more fundamental than making sure that the people in your region can find you. People are using and relying on search engines to get information on *local* businesses—and may or may not click through to those businesses' own websites. In fact, a whopping 25 percent of all searches are local-based, and this number is quickly growing. It used to be that any business that relied on local traffic made sure it was listed in the Yellow Pages. The name of the game today, however, is to make sure you're listed in local search engines.

See and Be Seen!

The top five places you need to add (or update) your contact information are:

- Google Places—*bit.ly/AddGoogleBusiness.*
- Yelp—*biz.yelp.com.*
- Facebook—*facebook.com/business.*
- Yahoo Local—*bit.ly/YahooBiz.*
- Bing Maps—*bingplaces.com/DashBoard.*

Google and Bing will verify your information by sending you a PIN code, either by phone or mail. Yahoo verifies its information internally.

You can just put in the basics, but you're better off filling out the listing completely. Every single one of the things you list (such as services, hours of operation, categories, etc.) acts like a keyword, which makes your listing search engine-friendly. To rank even higher, make sure to include your relevant terms in your description (including type of business, location, service area, and so on).

Contact Info Clarity Equals Customers

Although Google, Yahoo, and Bing try to correlate their own data with the information coming in from other sources, sometimes the details just don't match up. In these cases, a business may end up with multiple listings (and different contact details). Even worse, if the wrong contact information appears in enough other places on the web, the major search engines may think that the incorrect information is, in fact, correct. If your business is already listed, you'll need to make sure that the information is accurate.

If you need to change your listing, go to:

1. Google Places (Must be logged into Google.)
   - Edit Your Listing—*http://tinyurl.com/gplaceseditCOC1.*
   - Report A Problem—*http://tinyurl.com/gplacesreportCOC1.*
   - Report Verification Issue—*http://tinyurl.com/gplacesreportvCOC1.*

2. Yahoo Local

- Report Incorrect Information—*http://tinyurl.com/ yahooreportCOC1.*

- Contact Customer Care. (On the Report Incorrect Information page, click the button at the bottom of the page.)

3. Bing Maps

- Check Your Listing—*http://tinyurl.com/blistingCOC1.*

- Contact Support—*http://tinyurl.com/bsupportCOC1.*

Tip 33 Get Listed in Online Directories

Back in the day, every business owner knew their contact information would appear in print in the Yellow Pages. Online directories organize information the same way: by category. Unlike the practically extinct Yellow Pages (which has a standard format of business name, address, and phone number), the information actually displayed in most online directories is not standardized. Some directories feature paid advertising or return irrelevant listings.

Regardless of how your listing actually displays, though, online directories are of particular interest because they will all send your information to the three major search engines and numerous local and mobile search partners. Once you're in the directory system, your information becomes widely available across the numerous platforms your customers use.

Directory Do's and Don'ts

First things first: Make sure you're even listed! Not only are you becoming visible to a large audience of potential customers, but getting listed in directories will automatically help you achieve higher search rankings. Be very careful to list your information correctly. It is generally pretty easy to get listed, but can be quite difficult to change your business details.

Next, you'll want to verify that your business information is correct. This may seem like a big "duh," but being listed is pretty much pointless (and actually harmful) if it's feeding users incorrect contact information—actively routing interested customers into a frustrating black hole.

On many sites, your basic business information may already be listed, in which case, you'll need to "claim" your listing. If you search for your business, a link to claim your listing should be on the results page, usually toward the bottom of the page.

As of this publishing, there are many places to get listed for free—as well as a growing number of websites that call themselves "directories"—and the landscape is rapidly changing. You should add your business to the most popular free Internet yellow pages (IYPs):

- SuperPages—*http://tinyurl.com/spagesCOC1.*
- YellowPages—*http://tinyurl.com/ypagesCOC1.*
- BizJournals—*bit.ly/Add2BizJournals* (click on "Add Your Company").
- MagicYellow—*bit.ly/MagicYellowBiz.*

If you do a search for additional IYPs, you may find yourself confounded by hundreds of results. The truth is that many of these are powered by primary data sources that are not technically IYPs but, rather, the data providers behind them. As such, you should add your business to the following data sources as well:

- InfoUSA—bit.ly/infoUSAbiz.
- Localeze—http://tinyurl.com/localezeCOC1. (As of 2013, it costs to "add" your listing to their database. You may "claim" your listing for free if it is already in the directory.)

In September 2010, when behemoth Facebook got in on the local search game, it launched a "Facebook Places" check-in service (much like Google Places). Although it had 500 million users of its own, it had an additional 3 million local business "fan pages," that are now just business pages. So, in order to start out strong, Facebook Places was powered by Localeze.

Tip 34 Be Open to Reviews

 In addition to internet yellow pages and online directories (many of which have review functions), it's important that you make your business accessible to everyday reviewers. In fact, you should actively encourage your own customers to review your business.

First of all, it's a point of differentiation between you and your competitors. Searchers prefer businesses that have been reviewed. It adds legitimacy and credibility. Second, your reviews boost your odds of being found online. Although most search engines keep their search algorithms a secret, the general consensus of search engine optimization experts is that businesses with reviews score higher in search results. Third, knowing you're being reviewed helps keep you—and your staff—honest about the level of service you provide. Knowing you may be reviewed helps your staff treat every customer as that golden "secret shopper."

More Is More, in Terms of Reviews

There's a power in the number of credible reviews that you have: the more, the better. A large number of good reviews speaks volumes about the consistently good service and product you provide. And, the more reviews you have, the less each one counts in the big picture—meaning that less weight is accorded to the occasional neutral or even negative review.

Yet, sheer numbers aren't everything. Even having three to five good reviews will increase your search ranking. Consider this: no rankings means you're not even on the board. This means that the best business with no reviews will still be ranked below a crummy one-star business.

> Contrary to its early roots—as a young, snarky, meet-up kind of site—Yelp has become a force to be reckoned with. Data from 2010 revealed, 54 percent of Yelpers are over the age of 35. Furthermore, an impressive 62 percent make more than $60K annually.

Reviews Are Here to Stay (Like It or Not)

If you find yourself still hedging about proactively dealing with reviews, I understand what you're thinking. As much as you might agree with me that you need to be reviewed, it's still difficult to start the process when you have a nagging fear, a pit in the bottom of your stomach, grumbling, "What if they don't like me?"

Perhaps, like many, it stems from subliminal high school experiences—not wanting to put yourself out there for fear of rejection or scorn. Let me assure you, though: not only is it the right thing to do, it's something you *must* do. Unlike high school, with online reviews, you can confidently respond back, in a professional way, thereby improving your reputation. Furthermore, you don't really have a choice anymore. You will be reviewed whether you like it or not. So, you might as well become an active participant in the process.

The fact is, criticism is inevitable. No matter how outstanding your business is, there *will* be negative reviews. For most businesses, though, the positive reviews far outweigh the negative ones. But, as Yelp reps noted to me, some criticism can actually bolster the credibility of positive comments. "We understand that on a personal level, negative reviews can sting," they explained, "but if the reviews on Yelp were 100 percent positive, they would be 100 percent less trustworthy."[1]

By mid-2014, Yelpers around the world had written more than 61 million reviews, making Yelp the leading local guide for real word-of-mouth on everything from boutiques and mechanics to restaurants and dentists. In speaking with Yelp reps for a Long Beach Post article, they informed me that, contrary to common belief, Yelp reviews skewed overwhelmingly positive: Only about one in every seven reviews (or 15 percent) was negative. "Additionally," they noted, "our research indicates that users don't make decisions based on a single review, but, rather, focus on the big picture.[2]

Jump in Already

So, go ahead and add your business to the top four review-specific sites:

- Yelp—*biz.yelp.com.*
- Citysearch/InsiderPages—For free listing, manual add is the only option for new accounts. E-mail myaccount@ citygridmedia.com.
- ServiceMagic—*http://tinyurl.com/smagicCOC1.*
- Angie's List—*business.angieslist.com.*

Once you're listed, start encouraging your best customers and fans to participate in posting positive reviews—not just on the four sites above, but on any site that has a review function. (It's important to note that the review sites do not encourage businesses to solicit reviews, but honestly, there's no down side. You won't be blacklisted for asking good customers to review you well.)

Keep in mind that though your best client may not be a Yelp user and probably doesn't want to be bothered with setting up an account; she may routinely use YellowPages.com and might feel comfortable writing a review there. A simple e-mail requesting a review, with a link to your business's specific listing, may be all the encouragement your customers need to help you shine.

Tip 35 Respond to Your Reviews

Believe it or not, bad reviews can also present opportunity—a profound opportunity, in fact. In the previous sections, we've discussed the fact that many sites probably already have a listing of your business—whether it's correct or incorrect—and we've gone over the ways to update (or create) that listing. Now that you know you can be found, you may (or may not) be shocked to see that you're already being reviewed, and sometimes it's not all rainbows and fairy dust. Thus, it's time for us to have a slightly uncomfortable chat about responding to what's being said about you.

What I've found time and again is that most companies are incredibly scared of this process. Truth be told, no one enjoys feeling criticized. We tend to make excuses to avoid having to deal with it. You may say you don't have the time or resources to monitor everything being said about you. You may feel overwhelmed by it all. You may also have fear to engage with an anonymous reviewer—especially when the business doesn't have the luxury of being anonymous itself. A company has to put itself out there, and once it's "out there," it's out there for good. It's scary to think that an anonymous person could drag you through the mud, but even scarier to do nothing about it.

For many companies, it's daunting to think of all the different places online where people may be dishing out reviews. (For instance, far beyond Yelp and CitySearch, a random blogger may be trashing your business, and that would be a good thing to know.) Thus, a "cottage industry" (of sorts) has developed, with a host of new experts.

"Online reputation management" is a whole practice that has recently emerged to address the ways a company is seen and responded to on the web. Really, it's just a disciplined approach to noting what is being said about a business—and where—and then choosing whether or not to engage in the social discussion. It doesn't take an expert to manage your online reputation, though. The bottom line is this: you have the power to respond to both negative and positive reviews.

 My advice is to treat your reviews as if they were a suggestion box. If you had a suggestion box in your lobby, naturally, you'd want to read every slip in there. Then, you would choose how you wanted to respond to your customers' comments, ideas, suggestions, or critiques, without necessarily committing to contact every single customer.

Online reviews are really no different. In every individual circumstance, you actually have three choices:

1. Don't respond. You can choose to do nothing. (You need to realize, however, that choosing to do nothing is, in fact, a *choice*.) That's not necessarily a bad thing—as long as you're engaged on your end by reading the reviews and making adjustments in your business.

2. Respond to positive reviews, either publicly or privately. Reviewers are generally thrilled to get a response. Thus, replying to praise with a simple "Thank you, Mrs. Smith, for raving

about our luxurious pedicures" can help strengthen the bond with your existing customers.

Ultimately, though, you want to take it up a notch. Realize that there's an audience of "lurkers" looking at how you've responded. Choosing to post a response publicly is likely to make you seem like a kind and caring business to new customers. It also provides you with the opportunity to include keywords and marketing messages to future customers. ("Thank you, Mrs. Smith, for raving about our luxurious pedicures. Next time you come in, be sure to try our champagne service.")

Once you respond to a review, you're doing exactly what the Internet does best. That is, you're being interactive. You've started a discussion. And that is the cornerstone of social media.

3. Respond to negative reviews, either publicly or privately. It's natural to feel upset or angered by a negative review, and it's easy to take it personally. No matter how hurtful a negative review may be, however, it's up to you to squash those feelings of fear and rejection and put a helpful comment up in response.

If you've remedied a problem or addressed an issue, then it's worth posting publicly to let potential customers know that you've overcome what may be their objection. Perhaps it's as simple as "Thank you for bringing the state of our restrooms to our attention. We've added extra towels and are now monitoring cleanliness on an hourly schedule." Or maybe it's more vague, like "We listen to all of our customers and have an open-door policy. We encourage you to come talk to us to resolve your issues."

You can always answer in a professional way so that it elevates your reputation. As long as you show you're willing to make amends, it goes a long way with potential customers. It may even put you above a business with 100-percent-positive reviews.

Regardless of which road you decide to take, there are specific steps to follow. They're a little different for every site. On most review sites, you have the option of setting up a business owner's account. With this account, you can contact reviewers directly and/or respond to reviews with

You know you need to respond, but what's the best way to respond? You want to have an authentic voice, not come across as a lawyer, a robot, or a PR rep. Respond in your own voice in order to come across as "real." Of course, once you've crafted a thoughtful, personable reply, have someone else look it over before you post. Remember: once it's "out there," it's out there for good. Take a deep breath, press the "send" button, and start the discussion.

"owner comments." For example, in Yelp, on the bottom right-hand side of every review is a little button that says "Add Owner Comment." On other sites, such as Yahoo Local, anyone is able to respond to a review with their own comments—including you. On Google, simply click on the link that reads: "Respond publicly as the owner."

This is the real power of the review. Although they may seem unmanageable at first, you are really in control of your reviews—both good and bad. You may not be able to control what people say about you, but you can absolutely control how you respond.

Actually, you have a fourth option as well. It's a rare circumstance and can be difficult to address. If a review is truly fraudulent or severely inappropriate, however, you may need to take action. Contact the site owner to remove the comment completely from the system. Perhaps an inflammatory remark comes from a competitor, a former employee, a spammer, or an ex-girlfriend. Regardless of the source, each site has its own way of dealing with these issues. The best thing to do is simply contact the site owner directly. Either they'll point you to the right channel or investigate the issue personally.

You've taken some huge steps in the last five tips. You'll be listed higher in search engines, be found on local searches, create lasting bonds with your customers, and start discussions with new prospects online. You are now in control of your online reputation.

In the Real World: Kreme de la Kreme Nail Salon

Kreme de la Kreme Nail Lounge is an upscale nail salon in Long Beach, California. It's a "typical" small business in as much as it serves a local audience and relies on referrals and its reputation to thrive and grow.

Although the five-year-old boutique salon probably doesn't refer to it in technical terms, Kreme de la Kreme has really embraced the idea of "online reputation management." First of all, the business has filled out a Yelp profile in full; it offers complete information about the salon's specialties and hours as well as a website link, a company history, photos, and even a special offer. In addition, the salon's owner, Angela T., was quite active on Yelp, responding to user reviews—some of the good ones and all of the bad ones.

In the following example, Angela T. responds to a Good (four-star) review from Destiny G.

Review From Destiny G.

OK, so my review is not as an actual client but a witness...Since most of my weekends are spent in Long Beach I've been looking around for a place to get my nails done. I pass by KDLK every constantly as my boyfriend lives down the block and last Friday I decided to pop in. It was my daughter's birthday that day, she turned 3 and was excited with the idea of having her nails painted. I decided that since KDLK looked so cutesy it would be the perfect place to take her and get us some mani/pedis. Unfortunately since I didn't have an appointment and they were booked that idea was a bust. Upon learning of the special day, Angela who was just the sweetest, squeezed my daughter in for a quick mani complete with flower design, the perfect nail polish for a 3 year old (light pink and sparkly!), gave us some cupcakes and posed her for some pictures. My daughter could not have been happier and I am looking forward to coming in and pampering myself soon.

Comment From Angela T. of Kreme de la Kreme Nail Lounge

Thanks Destiny, it was so sweet, meeting you and your little princess, She was so excited to be there and so well mannered, we are looking forward to pampering you both soon. See you soon.

This is a great response because it's personable and encourages the customer to come back again. In addition, it tells new customers that Kreme de la Kreme is a place that remembers its clients and values repeat business.

Actually, just the fact that Angela responds *at all* positively affects someone deciding whether they want to visit the salon. Because of her interaction, she's perceived as a business owner that is conscious of the results of her services and is engaged with her customers.

Of course, you're not going to please all of the people all of the time. In fact, 10 percent of Angela's reviews are negative. However, because she's taken the steps to remedy specific issues—and posted her own comments about them—she's likely to be perceived as head and shoulders above salons without any owner comments.

In the following review, Angela responds to a Bad (one-star) review from Carol V.

Review From Carol V.

Overrated and way overpriced. My best friend made an appointment for me to get a minx the morning of my wedding. A Danielle did my minx. This was my first time getting a minx so I do not know if getting a dry assed manicure is protocol but in all my years getting regular manicures they have never not soaked my cuticles before removing them. So when Danielle didn't soak my hands and proceeded to push my cuticles down then remove them to say it was painful is an understatement. She also badly cut my middle and ring finger on my right hand and simply just wiped the blood and didn't bother to apologize or anything. Now I am on my honeymoon with a very badly infected ring finger. It still hurts 3 days after my wedding. This place is right down the street from me and I will NOT be going back. I'll also be sure to urge some friends of mine who run some long beach wedding blogs to not recommend this place and post pictures of my badly cut and infected nail because someone was to rushed and lazy to cut my cuticles correctly.

Comment From Angela T. of Kreme de la Kreme Nail Lounge

Because our salon goes to great lengths to provide the highest level of cleanliness and service, we take your comment very seriously, especially the claim that our services led to an infection. Please bring us the photographs of your infected finger so that we may evaluate them for purposes of compensating you for your discomfort during your honeymoon. The more troubling aspect is that your writing Yelp reviews on your honeymoon!

Angela really gets it right here by saying "we take your comments very seriously." That's really what a potential customer is looking for: to be heard. Ideally, though, Angela would have also talked about specific actions they take to avoid infections.

It's also important to note that humor and sarcasm doesn't come across well online; Angela's joke in her last sentence may have struck the wrong note with the reviewer and perhaps potential clients as well. Even so, the quip is true to her style.

In fact, Angela's responses aren't "perfect" by any means. Her replies don't always hit the nail on the head, but they are authentic and real. It's obvious that there's not a PR "machine" responding to her user reviews; it's really Angela. As an involved business owner, she realizes that it's more about the *discussion* than about answering perfectly.

Her responses to each individual user are certainly important in terms of the relationship that they create with that person, but ultimately Angela's responses are aimed at people who haven't yet been to the salon. So, while she may not be the most polished (except for her fingernails, of course), she accomplishes the most important thing, which is conveying to the potential customer that she cares.

When asked about her thoughts on the site, Angela notes that many of her clients come to her via Yelp and acknowledges that it's an important marketing tool—for *any* location-based business. Even so, despite Yelp's incredibly persistent efforts, Kreme de la Kreme does not pay for advertising on the site. Angela feels that her profile and comments are enough to keep customers coming in the door.

Her advice to other business owners is simple: "Wait a week before responding to any post," she says. "It gives you time to cool off." The secret to good responses, she notes, is to "be objective and professional"—sound advice for *any* customer relations effort.

Do: Include a product review system on your website, and utilize customer comments to vet unsatisfactory products and provide excellent follow-up service.

Don't: Undermine your company's trust and credibility by sanitizing those reviews, only allowing customers to view positive ratings.

Here, we'll look at the potential benefits you can derive from a different type of review. Instead of reviews of you and/or your business that might appear on other websites (like Yelp), I'm recommending that you offer your customers the option of reviewing your products on your own website.

Product reviews serve many positive business purposes, such as:

- Building credibility and trust.
- Providing additional product and usage information.
- Giving insight on unsatisfactory products.
- Improving your overall customer experience.

Product reviews provide consumers with a boatload of additional product information—all at zero additional cost to you! So let your customers give you something valuable back by providing a forum for their input.

In addition to giving an overall review, reviewers tend to go into detail about their use of the product and how well it met their personal needs. This is extremely valuable info that simple product descriptions just can't provide. In a customizable world, knowing whether a given shredder, for example, works especially well to pulverize credit cards may be precisely the bit of information that a customer wants to see before pulling the trigger and buying.

The bottom line is simple: Positive product reviews push conversion rates. So using an online review system is a definite *do*.

Get Candid With Customers

Consumer reviews are a form of trusted content, the kind we talked about in Chapter 6. In fact, according to Lightspeed Content, 47 percent of consumers rely on customer-generated product reviews on a company's website over those on social media or print media before deciding to buy.

The fact of the matter, according to eMarketer, is that a potential customer is way more likely to trust (up to 12 times more likely) another consumer's review over your own stellar product description.[3] That's probably due in large part to a perceived alignment of interests shared with a fellow consumer: they're both spending money and want proven value. You, on the other hand, as lovely as you are on the inside, are viewed as looking to make a sale.

Don't Sanitize Reviews and Undermine Consumer Trust

A review system offers a key way to build your company's credibility, especially with new customers. Nonetheless, some sellers balk, understandably wanting to maintain every appearance of product perfection, and are therefore uncomfortable with the idea of giving buyers free reign to post possibly negative reviews. But, perhaps paradoxically, customers are more likely to trust a company that has some bad product reviews on its website.

Why? Because no one and nothing is perfect. And seeing that a company refrains from masking or blocking less-than-perfect commentary—allowing customers to keep it real—builds trust in both the company and other positive reviews.

Embrace Bad Reviews and Use Them to Troubleshoot

You can look at the glass half empty and bemoan bad reviews. Or you can seize the opportunity presented by subpar reviews and take advantage of a very valuable silver lining.

First, poor reviews help you vet unsatisfactory products. By knowing that a problem exists, you have the ability to improve, replace, or remove that particular item from your inventory.

Second, and perhaps even more critically, bad reviews provide insight into suboptimal customer experiences—giving you the opportunity to provide excellent follow-up service with a potentially disgruntled customer. Contact unhappy customers and see how you can help further.

Chapter 8

Change Your Social Media Value

Eavesdropping on the Market

"Social business" is today's hot buzzword for good reason. "Social media," however, is a bit of a misnomer. The word "media" implies a one-way relationship, a "broadcast" or "push." In reality, it's all about the social relationship, an interactive back and forth, and the technology that enables it. Online interaction on a social level is a connection, a two-way conversation, many times (en masse) that mimics many of the best parts of our relationships offline. A growing number of today's consumers live and breathe in digital real-time, and expect this two-way relationship from their brands, products, service providers, and causes. Social media contains the conversation itself, which is an actual asset—just as valuable as those on your balance sheet (see Tip 13).

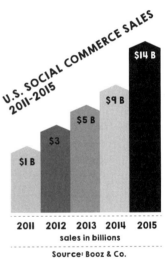

U.S. SOCIAL COMMERCE SALES 2011-2015

$1 B — 2011
$3 — 2012
$5 B — 2013
$9 B — 2014
$14 B — 2015

2011 2012 2013 2014 2015
sales in billions
Source: Booz & Co.

Many of us are immediately overwhelmed when we examine the breadth and depth of social media. Spend a second with the term "social media diagram" on Google Images and you'll instantly be presented with confusing infographics that try to neatly categorize all the platforms that exist. The universe likely includes things you didn't even fathom were social media, all creating sharable user-generated content like:

- Review sites.
- Blogs that allow comments.
- Comment aggregators that fuel cross-platform conversation (from Disqus to a Facebook plugin at the bottom of an article).

- Online directories where users contribute ratings (like GlassDoor.com's users rating their workplaces).
- Visual-driven places (from recipes and fashion on Pinterest to that awesome sunset you posted on Instagram).
- Social gaming (from the latest Facebook game craze to platform-driven communities, like Xbox).

> ### Are You Share-Worthy?
>
> Think of social as anything sharable. Sharable Assets = Value
>
> To engage is the start, but if you get a "share" from a trusted source (or, even better, 20 sources), it can make all the difference. In fact, Google rewards the type of dynamic user-generated content that social technology breeds, and arguably even more so if you use its social technologies (like YouTube and G+).

- Industry-specific conversations (Tripadvisor, Airbnb, and Travelzoo).
- Mobile app communities, sometimes within the apps themselves.
- Expert groups (on the likes of LinkedIn, Quora, or clarity.fm).
- Check-ins and reward systems.
- YouTube.
- Podcasts.
- Business networking and entrepreneur communities.
- Live conferences and online webinars.
- Couponing and daily deal sites.
- Hyper-local communities (like nextdoor.com).
- Shopping sites (from Etsy to Amazon and everything in between).
- All of the communities built around the technology that brought you social media in the first place.

Phew! That's just to name a few.

The danger of moving down this list is that it ends up being a huge paralyzer of action. Many people shut down or just ignore this space because they don't understand it. Furthermore, all of the constant changes lead to confusion. And hence, the opportunity opens for you, because you're starting to look at it all in the *context of the conversation*, not just content.

Tip 36 Mastering the Time and Space Continuum

"Mobile" is the rocket-fueled accelerating force that creates both time and location-sensitive exchanges. The context of time and space ("locale") is essential for understanding when and where you may choose to engage in social media.

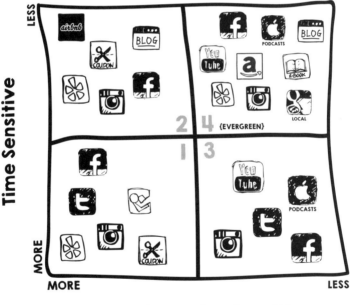

Space/Location Sensitive

1. Applications that allow for GPS-driven check-ins (like Yelp, Foursquare, and Facebook) act within the context of an exact place with an experience expiration date.

2. These applications allow for reviews and conversations about a particular business or location, but are not time-sensitive (such as the ratings and reviews on Google Local or AirBnB).

3. Other conversations are very real-time and not always location-specific (such as a rallying cry or fulfilling a need on Twitter or broadcasting a moment on Instagram).

4. "Evergreen" user-generated content that is posted for anytime viewing, listening, or reading, becomes a growing database of permanent assets that serve as conversation starters, attracting influencers and actual sales, in perpetuity. This last group runs the gamut from blog posts, to YouTube videos, to podcasts, to viral Facebook posts, e-books, coupon threads, Amazon reviews, and much, much more.

Conversations = Your Market

As a business, it is paramount to understand how your target audience finds you and behaves. Social media pioneer Brian Solis calls this the "experience flow" and speaks about Generation C, the connected customer. Generation C expects:

-   Information to find them (they'll put out "the ask" on Twitter, Facebook, etc.).

-   On-demand marketing, sales, and service, 24/7.

-   Constant reassurance, as they're never quite sure they made the right decision.

In Chapter 1, we created personas that looked beyond just demographics and psychographics. In creating a persona (or, the story that gives dimension to your consumer), you've got to know your customers' interests, what cause drives them, and most importantly, where they hang out online. Go there! Not a scattershot, but there-there. Chances are, there is a conversation that you could add value to—right now.

Of course, it's okay to "stalk" for a while and get to know the lay of the land. But, you'll know you have arrived when you strategically join a conversation with active participants that are hungry for your voice's value-add, and you'll naturally start attracting them to what you are selling. As Brian Solis stated:

Not only are markets now conversations, the audience is no longer passive or static. Their attention is no longer described in terms of eyeballs, traffic, or time onsite. Audiences are now connected and democratized. The power of influence is shifting where it is not owned but, instead, *shared*. We are, in fact, faced with an informed and connected audience that now has an audience with audiences of its own. We are not just talking to people. We are presented with an opportunity to talk with and through them, activating networks, sparking conversations and engagement, and building relationships that offer mutual value.[1]

Tip 37 Eavesdrop to Find the Social Butterflies

Twitter is truly the place to gauge the pulse of the local conversation. When you (and other locals) are active on Twitter, you can really get immersed in immediate feedback.

To build a healthy following of locals, start following socially active:

- Restaurants.
- Event organizers.
- Promoters.
- DJs.
- Chamber, Rotary, and local networking organizations.
- Offline traditional "relationship managers" (like Realtors, accountants, and insurance agents).
- Local non-profits.
- Anyone that Tweets live from local events.
- Local bloggers (Patch.com is a good starting place to find these folks).

Once you've found the locals that also follow these connectors, follow *them*.

Use advanced Twitter search to:

- Search local-based hashtags and key phrases.

- Find active users to listen in on (and, eventually, have conversations with).

It's like you overheard someone at a party and chimed in. The etiquette is the same; you wouldn't just interrupt someone with a sales pitch, but a helpful comment would be quite welcome.

Tip 38 Build Your Social Asset Empire

Time is money. And nowhere is this truer than within a small business, with limited human resources. As discussed throughout this book, despite fewer resources, small businesses still have to engage online in a consistent and purposeful way across many different platforms in order to compete. You *cannot* accomplish this unless you consolidate your efforts and create a repository of approved materials that can be accessed— at your discretion—by your team.

Chances are, the pieces you use to tell your story will be spread across devices. To that end, I recommend a Dropbox folder, dedicated to housing your digital assets. Large corporations have used shared folders and servers for ages. Today, any size of business can enjoy the same benefits of sharing data. Flip back to Tip 13 for a full list of the types of assets that will put you out front if you begin actively cataloging them.

In order to tell your story, you'll have to gather the pieces that will be part of the social posts that you put out into the world. These pieces ("digital assets") are the building blocks of engagement, trust, and inbound links to your website.

Some of that content will be "evergreen," meaning it won't have a specific expiration date. To facilitate evergreen content creation—and have assets on hand for speedy real-time responses—you can stock your Dropbox "asset locker" with approved materials such as:

- Photos (lifestyle shots, product images, behind the scenes, events, #TBT "throwbacks," stock photography, etc.).
- Your logo.
- Your creative projects.
- Inspirational quotes from others (ideally overlaid on an eye-catching image).

- PR releases.
- Media-approved stats.
- Press clippings.
- Approved quotes from inside your organization.
- Downloaded podcasts.

How many people do you trust on your social team to tell your story? At the very least, your customers and brand ambassadors are the directors of the team. Their user-generated content is key: anything that your customers write (or photograph) about you or your products (including reviews, rants, and raves) can be studied and repurposed. Make sure you capture it! Keep track of:

- User testimonials.
- Screen captures from review and social sites.
- User photos, videos, podcasts, infographics, or any other UGC (user generated content).

Evergreen Content

This is a standard component of magazine content, and can be crafted in advance and/or reworked from past materials. (Think of the standard holiday-themed fare, which is usually written, edited, and approved by July of each year.) For ChunkofChange.com, my own Dropbox "Social Assets" folder includes:

- Lifestyle shots.
- Headshots.
- Book goodies.
- Events.
- Creative materials.

- Family photos.
- Random stuff.
- Thought leaders.
- COC logos.
- UGC (User-generated content).

Get Visual

Here are five places to get free or cheap images:

1. Create your own! You'll own those photos outright. Just be sure to get model releases from any subjects depicted—even your employees—especially if you plan to use those pics in advertisements.

2. DollarPhotoClub.com is one of my favorite sites because, yes, every photo is just $1.

3. Visit iStockPhoto.com for a long-standing, broad selection—lots of royalty-free options.

4. The Library of Congress online has many historical and news-worthy images that are part of the public domain and can be sourced through local libraries.

5. If you're trying to create an infographic or cartoon, edit photos, or create visually interesting marketing materials, check out Fiverr.com, where you can hire someone for a limited gig for a whopping $5.

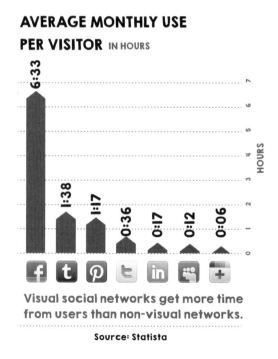

AVERAGE MONTHLY USE PER VISITOR IN HOURS

Visual social networks get more time from users than non-visual networks.

Source: Statista

Utilize Video Content

We've discussed the power of digital video content at length in Chapters 4 and 5, but it bears reiteration here: whenever you can, incorporate video into your social media materials. It will have a major impact on current customers and potential customers who live (and spend) in the online universe. Beyond that, posting video content to social media streams allows you to gauge interest (almost) in real-time, through Likes, Pins, and re-Tweets.

How Tagging Video Content Can Have Unexpected Consequences

Video marketing expert Katie Covell offers a word of warning about posting video content: "Tag with caution." Tags send videos shooting to the top of search results, which *can* be great. But tags can also push less-polished videos to the top of the search heap as well.

To ensure you put your best foot forward in search results, Covell recommends properly sorting your content. This may entail *not* tagging content that you want to stay put on your website or blog.

Try Googling yourself and your business to see the results that rise to the top, particularly for search-buoyant video content. You may be surprised, possibly even dismayed, at the order in which your videos appear. If so, review the way the content is sorted and watch out for loose tags!

Tip 39 Let the Love In

One of my favorite Theodore Roosevelt quotes came to me by way of awesome vulnerability advocate and social researcher Brenee Brown:

> It is not the critic who counts; not the man who points out how the strong man stumbles, or where the doer of deeds could have done them better. The credit belongs to the man who is actually in the arena, whose face is marred by dust and sweat and blood...who at the best knows in the end the triumph of high achievement, and who at the worst, if he fails, at least fails while daring greatly.

Think of the last person that you ad-mired—and how vulnerable that person was. We tend to admire vulnerability in others, but view it as weakness in ourselves. And, yet, it is exactly that vulnerability that leads to the connection that social media is all about. We all know the Facebook friend who only shows you the mask of the perfect family. Do you feel more connected to that person or the friend who pokes fun at herself for showing some sort of parenting "fail"?

Judge, Jury, and Executioner

You have "haters" right now, lurking around the Internet, saying nega-tive things about you—somewhere. The more active you are in the social sphere, the more the trolls come out to play. Do you run away and hide? No. That would also exile you from all the other connections that are to your benefit.

So, here is the challenge: how do you let the "haters" move on through, while carrying on your positive online conversations? Open up the conver-sation. Companies that open up their Facebook walls to uncensored con-versation are viewed more favorably than those that try to "control" happi-ness propaganda.

#FAIL

You may not know Twitter etiquette, have the best grammar, or feel like you look great on video. Even so, you must resist the need to put up only things that are polished, finished, and perfect. In truth, anything too "slick" will be viewed with skepticism anyway.

It's really consistency that is key. This is especially true of social media. Some companies post for a few weeks and, once the novelty wears off, they're done with it. We've all seen the blogs where the "so excited about my first post" turns into "sorry, I haven't posted for a while." If you just com-mit to an ongoing presence, you'll already be in the top 10 percent. In order to stay competitive, keep the topics fresh and keep the conversation going.

What the Research Says
With Dr. Norah Dunbar

Using social media can be a huge boon to your business because it can get your brand noticed by customers you might not normally reach. But, you must remember that, though you can set up a Facebook site for your business and post videos to YouTube, social media is indeed "social." This means anyone can comment about your business on social media, opening the door for both positive and negative commentary by others. One of my favorite examples is the song "United Breaks Guitars" by singer Dave Maxwell. After a negative customer service experience with United Airlines, he posted a protest video about it on YouTube, and it went viral immediately, was named by *Time* magazine one of the Top 10 viral videos of 2009, and was a public relations nightmare for United. Researchers Corstjens and Umblijs investigated the impact of social media activities on the actual performance of brands in the market in an ominously titled article "The power of Evil" in the *Journal of Advertising Research*. They distinguish between three types of social media activities relating to the advertisement of a brand:

- Type 1 is induced and encouraged—but not paid for—by brand owners.

- Type 2 is produced by consumers for brand owner at the brand owner's request.

- Type 3 is generated by consumers or communities that are neither paid for nor induced by brand owners. Maxwell's song about United fits into this category.

The authors examined a number of different product categories and accounted for other factors such as consumer confidence and traditional marketing used by the various brands. Then, they looked at the impact of both positive and negative Type 3 commentary on a variety of social media sites, and then looked at how it affected sales, subscriptions, and other market indicators. Their results revealed that the effect of negative commentary outweighed the positive messages. In other words, the damage caused by negative social media relations played a bigger role in a company's success than positive messages from fans. The authors warn that marketing professionals should no longer view customers as "targets" or advertising messages as one-way. Customers have been given a voice through social media and aren't afraid to use it. In your business, staying aware of what customers are saying about your company on social media and responding to those messages quickly is vitally important.

Tip 40 Build Your Audience

Chances are, your industry has a trade show, event, or conference with speakers that are viewed as authorities in your sphere. Can you connect with them in the real world to create a social asset you can use online?

Mike Stelzner of Social Media Examiner did just that when he went out to conferences with his own low-budget camera crew to interview any thought leader that would give him 10 minutes. He then edited those videos to 15-minute segments that he doled out over time on his blog.

Soon enough, the sharable content spread to the audience that already followed those particular thought leaders. Today, Social Media Examiner has more than 250,000 subscribers and Stelzner is now a top influencer in his own right, surpassing many of those he first interviewed.

Likewise, John Lee Dumas saw an opportunity to create a *daily* podcast by interviewing entrepreneurs with a following. His "-est" was that there was a fascinating "How I Made It" story to share 365 days a year. He interviewed eight thought leaders every Monday and then released those podcasts, once a day. He conducted close to 700 interviews in less than two years, and many of those executives he interviewed have shared those podcasts with their audiences.

John pulls in more than $200,000 a month, and happily shares his P&L on eofire.com in a transparent way, along with a monthly podcast that anyone can listen in on. It is his most-listened-to show all month.

Care More Online Than the Other Guy

Social media success is not about the number of users; it's about the number of true influencers and your advocates that are thrilled to be connected with you. Putting yourself out there doesn't really mean much unless your information is passed on. Too many businesses broadcast information, one-way, with no idea of the conversation that is going on around them. The way that you build online relationships is by building goodwill, by listening and showing empathy.

One of the best ways to show you care is by vetting all the available choices out there for your audience. There is a huge demand for curated content because we now live in a world where there is an anxiety of choices and true unhappiness in having to choose anything. Using your product, service, or cause's uniquely expert lens to help others in their decision-making process is valuable.

There are paid social media tools you can look to measure the buzz, keep track of your competitor's conversations, and pinpoint the influencers in your industry (such as saleforce.com's Radian6).

In the Real World: Brand New Instagrammer Finds Social Media Success With MFsox

If the story of how Scott Green got his specialty sock business, MFsox (short for Multi-Functional Socks), off the ground doesn't inspire you as to the business potential of social media, then nothing will.

Despite having never used Instagram prior to launch, Scott has used that platform (along with Facebook) as his sole advertising tools. Almost immediately, Scott amassed more than 400 followers and sold more than 300 pairs of socks. Not too shabby, considering that Scott started his solo business while also working a full-time job.

MFsox Rocks the #Hashtags

Green launched @MFsox in 2013, selling American-made knee-high socks with motivational mottos to hardcore fitness fanatics. Given the distinct target market, it didn't take long for the gym rats to post pictures of themselves proudly wearing their own MFsox, while pushing through their grueling Crossfit workouts, training sessions, and marathons.

Hashtags proved a key advertising tool, helping Green tap into the pockets of potential customers like veins of gold. From there, Green rode

the wave of the domino effect, with hashtags opening the door to individuals within his target market, and their purchases and subsequent posting of themselves in MFsox opening even more doors.

"Hashtags are half the battle," Green noted. "Numerous hashtags in relation to my product and other key fitness-related words helped draw attention to my product."

For example, Green would utilize an array of descriptors for every photo uploaded to the MFsox Instagram account (such as #mfsox #girlswholift #crossfit #getfit #madeintheusa #sweatmore). This would automatically organize his photos with those of other Instagram users using a matching hashtag—connecting Green and MFsox to members of their target audience. "Instagram allows me to have a direct link to a web store for people to order, so once I draw someone's attention to my page, I feel like it's one step closer to selling my socks."

Social Media Cross-Pollination

"The other trick," Green added, "was trying to get other people and companies to help promote my socks." When you're a one-man-band, customer word of mouth and business co-promotion can make or break your launch.

Green paid it forward to start the ball rolling. "Posting pictures while wearing t-shirts and using other products that are in the same target market helped for cross-marketing. People and companies would be excited to post and repost pictures of their products, while my socks would be visible as well. People would see the socks, start following us, and, in some cases, order our product."

By seeing social media as a time- and cost-effective marketing tool, and consistently updating Instagram and Facebook feeds to build a community of followers, Green has single-handedly managed to bring his unique product line to market.

Online Cross Promotion Crash Course

- Identify your target market(s).
- Observe their other preferred brands and products.
- Take action photos showing those brands along with your goods.
- Post on Instagram with hashtag name check. #tooeasy

DO **this** not **that**

Do: Use podcasts to find tools, resources, and the beginnings of your community.

Don't: Get lost in the sea of social media confusion.

I'd like you to sit with the idea of an interactive audience that self-selects into the topics that are important to them. Then, I'd like you to picture yourself as either an active member of that exact niche conversation or, as a leader of it.

"Why *podcasts*?" you may ask. "Aren't those soooo 2005?"

No!

The Bluetooth integration of my smartphone with my car, home system, and directly into my earphones—on demand—has me connected wherever I am. Most importantly, the medium itself feels intimate. When I'm at the gym, listening to an entertainer or business luminary, I start to feel like I know them. Take that feeling, mix in iTunes and the growth of other "radio apps," and sprinkle in the ease of sharability, and you have a trifecta that has elevated podcasts into the ears of a loyal audience—that wants more.

In order to build an audience for your product, service, or cause, I believe you should first consider being part of one by following the dots, starting with podcasts or radiocasts that speak to you and your market. Here are some steps to follow:

1. Choose your app of choice on your smartphone, such as iTunes or Stitcher.

2. Have fun and explore niches that relate to your industry, locale, or stuff that makes you feel like it is talking to you.

3. Go beyond the podcast to the online communities that the audience lives on. Where are they the most active? Most likely there will be a blog powered by Disqus comments, Facebook group, or Linked in group where you can find helpful folks on a similar journey.

Change Your Mobile Presence

Going SoLoMo (Social, Local, and Mobile)

Mobile phones in America have reached full saturation. In fact, two-thirds of us now use smartphones. Tasks that were once annoying to attempt on our phones are now second-nature. We are increasingly seeing e-mails on our mobile devices first, and using what's in our hands as the primary search tool for any real-time want. More than half of all smartphone users check their social networks on their mobile devices daily. Younger generations are using their mobile devices as the chief way they digest content, make purchasing decisions, and connect transparently with anyone and everyone—not just friends.

So, I beg you, unlock your idea of what you think mobile is. You already know it's not just a phone.

Fingers First

By thinking of your mobile users first, you get all the benefits (and none of the calories) of a bloated desktop interface. Taking a moment to concentrate on how mobile users will use their fingers to interact with information on a smaller screen allows you to focus on what to present first in an easier-to-navigate, without-a-mouse kind of way.

At the very least, everything gets bigger (text, buttons, navigation elements, etc.), which causes you to embrace constraints and really focus on what is important.

This chapter hopes to accomplish a lot more than simply encouraging you to have a mobile strategy. I want you to zoom out and see beyond today's set of mobile channels (i.e., text, phone, web, and apps). Instead, start looking at mobile technologies as a natural extension of wants and needs.

Mobile Evolution and Why It's Relevant to Local Business

In 2009, Foursquare introduced everyone to the "check-in." With more than 5 billion check-ins and counting, it now has the world's largest database of this behavior: where people are, where they broadcast their check-in, and what they like.

What does that mean for the future? Let's say you own a pizza parlor and there is a hungry potential customer nearby, "George." Right now if George uses Yelp, his search will be sorted by the top 10 nearby pizza joints.

George can sort by price or general type of food, but Yelp doesn't know George has a gluten intolerance. Let's now spice up your story and say that a part of your pizza restaurant's "-est" (see Chapter 1) is its delicious, gluten-free crust.

In waltzes the newest Yelp competitor, Swarm (Foursquare's newest mobile app), to blow your mind. On the Swarm mobile app, George is automatically drawn to your pizza place because Swarm already knows his gluten-free preference based on his behavior and leads him there. It'll also share George's location in a less-creepy way than the too-exact-for-comfort "find my phone" pin-dot, and draw folks from his social sphere to your establishment—just because George digs it.

Well, even if Swarm doesn't survive the mobile competition by the time you read this, its main idea will. Automatic location, preference, and social sharing is here to stay.

What if We Don't Need People to Check In Anymore?

"Back in 2009, declaring your location was a necessity, primarily because phones didn't have the power to reliably pinpoint a user, and Foursquare didn't have much data on what venues were nearby. By 2014, however, both the technology and the data have finally come of age."

—Foursquare CEO Dennis Crowley on launching Swarm

Once upon a time—a whole 20 years ago—people knew where they were going before they left the house. They *had* to; they didn't have cell phones to look up information on the fly. Now, people rely on their phones when they're out and about to orient them as to what and who is available in their immediate vicinity; at home, they're consuming curated content and sharing it via mobile, while watching their Smart TV.

Google places a premium on having a mobile focus, even "penalizing" those with websites that don't think of mobile first. Industry blog SearchEngineLand warns, "Around 40% of time spent online is on mobile devices now, and this percentage is only likely to grow. So, make sure your site is optimal for those devices. Google has stated that failure to optimize for mobile can now impact your rankings."[1]

Making your website optimal for mobile can be as simple as using a "responsive" template that adjusts content for the device it's being viewed on, or a lengthier exercise that makes you pare down exactly what you want folks to see on mobile first as a separate experience. Basically, if you're not optimized for mobile yet, you will be—soon.

Tip 41 Think of Your Website in Mobile Terms

Mobile has surpassed desktop and tablet as the number one way people look at their e-mail—and web browsing is not far behind. "By 2017, according to a forecast by research firm eMarketer Inc., sales made on mobile devices will hit $41 billion in the U.S. Yet just 8.8% of small business retailers sell via mobile commerce. Just as surprising: Nearly half of all small businesses lack a website and, of those that do have a site, most don't bother with a mobile-friendly version, StatisticBrain says."[2]

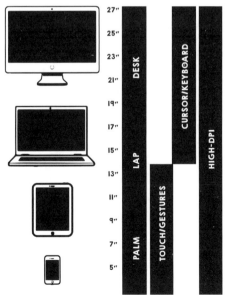

> **Responsive Web Design (RWD)**
>
> A web development approach geared toward an optimal viewing experience of one website that dynamically adjusts to both the screen size and the orientation of the device being used to view it.

Your website may look fantastic on your desktop, but how does it look when you load it on your phone? What happens when a fudgy finger controls the action (instead of a mouse)? And, in the future, how will it load on someone's wearable device, when their eyes are controlling the action?

If your online home base isn't optimized for mobile use, you may be shooting your business in the foot. If your beautiful site won't load, or the page size and content make it frustrating to pinch to view on a small screen, your potential lead will disappear. And, soon, you'll start to disappear from search results as well.

For developers, there has been a movement to standardize how websites are made for mobile. "User context" is all the buzz, or how to present information in the most helpful way, depending on what the user is expecting from it.

Streamline Your Current Site

If you already have a website up and running, but haven't optimized it for mobile at all, there are some simple steps you can take to maximize your site's translation to a mobile device. Google has some best practices suggestions, which focus on specific ways to streamline, including removing features that require certain plugins (like Adobe Flash, which isn't viewable on iPhone devices or more recent Android devices).

> **Want Mobile-Friendly on the Cheap?**
>
> A RWD template that you customize with branded graphics and content on a Wordpress platform is proving to be a very cost-effective route for the DIY crowd. Start at themeforest.net (search "Wordpress responsive") to see options that may work for your business type.

RESPONSIVE WEBSITE AS VIEWED ON MULTIPLE DEVICES

TABLET

MOBILE

DESKTOP AT 1024 PIXELS WIDE

DESKTOP AT 1580 PIXELS WIDE

Appears at right when widest.

One-and-Done With Responsive Web Design

Some businesses find it cost- and time-effective to have one website that is custom designed to appear properly in both computer and mobile platforms. Although you may be looking at a $5,000 to $25,000 build out, depending on your needs, the joint approach can save lots of time and money in the long term, as only one site will need to be updated or modified to make changes in both mediums.

Solo Mobile Site

Many experts suggest that the most cost-effective way to configure your website for mobile is *not* to configure your website at all. Rather, it may be easier to create a separate mobile site altogether. In fact, after build out, a 10-page mobile site could run as little as $13 a month.

Independent Mobile App

The state-of-the-art is moving at lighting speed in terms of app design and accessibility for entrepreneurs. In the past year alone, many new solutions have been offered so that non-tech folks can design their own apps, or hire programmers at more competitive prices. As such, an in-house app might be an avenue to explore, depending on your business. Keep in mind, however, that failures in functionality can turn potential customers into mobile maniacs, who will bail on a bug-ridden app in a heartbeat. Additionally, as app-centric as the mobile world is right now, we may be hitting a point of overwhelm with the sheer number of available app offerings. Adding a new, single-function app designed solely for one shopping experience may not appeal to folks looking to streamline their overall app experience.

**What the Research Says
With Dr. Norah Dunbar**

Whenever a new technology comes along, there's always a steep learning curve for businesses that try to use it to market their products, and mobile phones are no different. Early marketing efforts on phones attempted to mimic the strategies that have worked on desktop computers, but small screen devices like smartphones and mini-tablets are a different vehicle and should be treated differently. Harvard Business Professor Sunil Gupta suggested in a 2013 article in *Harvard Business Review* that ads on mobile phones don't work for the following three reasons:

1. Users don't like them because they are intrusive and interfere with their activity more than when they are on a desktop.

2. The ads pop up in unexpected places because there's no right margin for ads like on Facebook and other applications on a desktop.

3. Due to the "fat finger effect" people click on them accidentally so it's difficult to tell when they are really effective and result in real customers.

Gupta suggests that as we advance in our understanding of how consumers use mobile phones, then our understanding of how to best use them for marketing purposes will evolve as well. He suggests that creating apps is a way to reach audiences rather than ads because they can (a) add convenience because of their mobility, (b) offer unique value not available in other platforms, (c) provide social value, (d) offer incentives such as free mobile minutes or coupons, and (e) entertain with games or engaging apps. Though building apps might not be what you have in mind for your own marketing plan, using these principles when designing sites or ads for your mobile customers is a good way to make your mobile marketing more appealing.

Tip 42 Using the Marriage of Local and Mobile to Your Advantage

We search on our mobile devices in real-time, all around us, a lot. Not even Google can keep up. In 2012, for those that had smartphones, 84 percent used Google as *the* place to go. Today, however, because mobile is becoming a place that is so specialized, consumers are increasingly seeking a customized, faster app to search for what they need. The biggest indicator of this behavior shift is the growth of Yelp. In terms of revenue growth from mobile ads, it's quickly gaining traction. This shift in consumer behavior is a telling sign, pointing to an opportunity for using mobile as a customer magnet.

If you have a brick-and-mortar, consider mobile geo-location solutions like:

- Ads that show up on Google, YP, Yelp, or other networks that allow you to promote your business when a potential customer is near.
- QR Code integration on your signage and ads that allows users to scan for an incentive.
- Apps that broadcast "check-ins" or automatically ping a user's current location at your establishment.
- Twitter and Instagram posts hashtagged consistently from a local focus (#city #businessname #neighborhood #event).
- Specialized apps.

Furthermore, use Twitter, Instagram, and other social tools to:

- Identify customers within the area.
- Build an audience by conversing with locals.
- Consistently share specials, funny messages, and a story to round out the social conversation.
- Find social friends.
- Encourage brand ambassadors to post and share their experience (reaching yet another layer of nearby potential customers).

Instagram, recently growing past 100 million users, is a particularly powerful tool, as it naturally combines mobile with photo sharing. The whole "picture is worth a thousand words" worked for NYC's Comodo Restaurant, which set up a user-generated "Instagram Menu" with hashtag #comodomenu. Truly embracing digital marketing, the restaurant put the announcement out via a one-minute YouTube video, which spread locally and organically when diners shared it with their Instagram followers.

Tip 43 Groupon, Group Off: Use Daily Deals the Right Way

Daily deals have become less fashionable in recent years, mainly due to oversupply and the fatigue of the daily e-mails. Even so, the mobile experience has added an intriguing new component: knowing that customers are nearby and can be lured in locally, with an offer. Whether your business provides meals, sells merchandise, or offers services, it's possible to fashion some type of attractive incentive deal or discount to bring in new business.

Groupon is the biggest player in the daily deal market, with more than 45 million active users buying at least one deal in the past 12 months. As the company has grown, we've all seen some of the drawbacks of the super-couponing systems. In fact, Groupon itself is shying away from what made it famous (namely, those time-sensitive crazy daily deals) and moving toward multi-day deals available to anyone—no subscription necessary.

Living Social, the other large player in the daily deal space, is following suit by shifting users to their website and mobile app. There, shoppers browse for deals from local merchants that pique their interest.

Daily deal sites have long-enticed business owners with the promise of:

- Major advertising via massive outreach to a huge e-mail list.
- Reaching different and previously unidentified demographics.
- Securing new customers, who have been introduced to the business via the daily deal.

Unfortunately, a lot of retailer experiences have not synced up with these promises. Like, not at all. Here's why:

1. **Daily deal customers are often in the "always looking for a deal" demographic.** This means that they only buy when there's a discount—and won't return unless they get another coupon. Ultimately, there's no viable repeat business.

2. **You can accidentally poach from your existing clientele.** Converting a full-price customer to a half-price customer is not good economics, but that's exactly what can happen. Once your

full-price customers see half-price customers, they'll figure out how to pay half price, too.

3. **Daily deals negatively impact service.** New customers want to be impressed, but scores of coupon-carrying customers can cause a decrease in customer service in three ways.

   • Your business gets overly busy, and handling the influx of people becomes problematic.

   • Your staff isn't incentivized to give top-quality service to people demanding the best but only paying half.

   • And, either way, those customers slam you on Yelp.

Troubleshooting Daily Deals

It doesn't have to be "all bad." Here's how to do it right:

1. Don't create an arbitrary deal or discount without considering the actual cost, which must include the middleman's take.

2. Don't offer too many daily deals. If anyone can get the discounted price at any time, why wouldn't they?

3. Offer deals for overstock only. Daily deals are a fantastic way to move unwanted merchandise.

4. Limit the deal to something signature, but more cost-effective (like a specific lunch item).

5. Limit your deal offering to people outside of your main demographic areas to avoid poaching regulars and focus on completely new folks.

6. When formulating your deal, expect people to try to take advantage of it. Create a well-thought-out program, and have *some* kind of system in place to monitor coupon redemption (or, more accurately, re-redemption or over-redemption).

7. Hand out a flyer to your daily dealers that promises 20 percent off a future purchase if they sign up for your newsletter or follow you on social media, so they feel like they're getting yet another "deal."

8. People won't become repeat customers through a daily deal alone. So, treat your deal as a loss leader, but be clear what the later sell will be. It can be a discount club, a buy-two-get-one-free, a swag bag, or whatever else works.

9. Many retailers don't realize they can try to negotiate with the daily deal company. It never hurts to ask for a bigger percentage of the deal, especially after you've garnered success with previous deals.

Tip 44 Forget Location, Location, Location

The advent of mobile and social, tied together, is allowing for cheaper rents and unique situations wherein location is not the end all, be all.

Recently, I stopped into a decidedly hipster coffee shop—called Lord Windsor—in a fairly hidden (but supremely charming) Long Beach, California, neighborhood. While there, I spoke with local coffee roaster and owner Wade Windsor, who admitted that his heavy residential corner location, sans street parking, is a challenge. "Isolation is good for charm," he noted, "but not so much for foot traffic."

Luckily, the craft coffee community has a strong presence online and Lord Windsor is a favorite of the craft coffee aficionados. "When we first opened, I didn't really care for social media, to tell you the truth," Windsor shared. "But, then, I was blown away by how many people came to us, outside the immediate radius, saying they saw us on Instagram."

You Got to Have Friends

Orn Hansen is a clothing boutique with 23,870 Instagram followers that fancies itself a "Vintage + American Made General Store." The store's modern-meets-organic vibe is not in a premier location, like trendy Melrose in Hollywood, but one block down from Lord Windsor, on the same sleepy downtown Long Beach street.

Orn Hansen's Instagram photos are a constantly changing, beautiful magazine spread that tell a curated story about the retailer. As owners Robby Roda and Rodelle Bas put it, "It's all of us, here together. We try to promote together, we try to do things together. I think we're creating a story...with the brands we carry."[3] Part of that story is sticking to "keep it local" by including locally sourced products. They also connect well with the audiences of the brands that they carry. Instagram snapshots of gift suggestions tag brands they carry.

Bas told the *Long Beach Post*, "Sometimes people are genuinely surprised when they come here and realize that most things in here are made in California and everything is made in America. Y'know, we still make great things in this country and right here in Long Beach—and our shop is proof." Pretty cool UVP there if you ask me.

As of this writing, the boutique moved their physical shop location to their native Portland with no fear of losing audience. Orn Hansen didn't skip a beat. After all, their most valuable asset—26,000+ active Instagram followers—didn't have to be re-located. They live on the owner's mobile device.

To attract customers to your out-of-the-way, or online only, location using Instagram:

- Team up with like-minded brands, other local shops, and causes.

- Hashtag it up and tag away.

- Add to the picture story in a way that projects your UVP (e.g., Orn Hansen's post of a vintage poster reading "Buy American Goods So It Won't Be Bye-Bye America").

- Interact and provide reinforcement that your customers made the right choice.

- Encourage your followers to show off their purchases or experience.

Tip 45 Learn How Generations Y and Z Use Mobile

Generation Y (or "Millennials") and Generation Z (those born between 1992 and 2010) have become known as "the silent generation." Why "silent"? Well, when was the last time you saw a Y or Z actually *call* someone on a phone? One recent U.S. study, on the other hand, found that kids in grades 7 to 12 spent roughly 95 minutes a day texting.

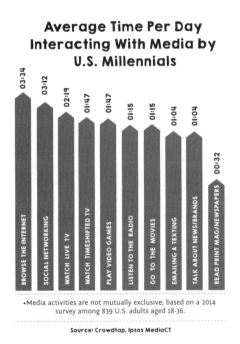

Average Time Per Day Interacting With Media by U.S. Millennials

BROWSE THE INTERNET	03:34
SOCIAL NETWORKING	03:12
WATCH LIVE TV	02:19
WATCH TIMESHIFTED TV	01:47
PLAY VIDEO GAMES	01:47
LISTEN TO THE RADIO	01:15
GO TO THE MOVIES	01:15
EMAILING & TEXTING	01:04
TALK ABOUT NEWS/BRANDS	01:04
READ PRINT MAG/NEWSPAPERS	00:32

•Media activities are not mutually exclusive; based on a 2014 survey among 839 U.S. adults aged 18-36.

Source: Crowdtap, Ipsos MediaCT

As digital natives, GenZs:

- Think beyond engagement.
- Want to have conversations with their brands.
- Expect information to come to them through social networks.
- Are less likely to travel and get out of the house.
- Put a lot of thought into their online personas.
- Believe in personal brands.

Consider this:

- 25 percent of Generation Z gets connected (by checking their e-mail, text messages, and/or social media) within five minutes of waking up.
- 46 percent are connected online for 10 or more hours a day.
- 100 percent are connected for at least one hour a day.

A 2014 Ipsos Media survey of 839 Millennials showed an average of roughly 18 hours of their day spent engaged with media, often viewing multiple devices simultaneously. Thus, the question isn't whether younger generations will hear your message. Rather, it's whether they'll listen and share it.

In the Real World: The University of MMA Uses Strategic Approach to Secure Daily Deal Success

Daily deals can prove disastrous for some businesses. But, when entrepreneurs approach the experience armed with expectations about the potential pros and cons (see Tip 43), are willing to commit to the trial-and-error process, and keep their focus on their big-picture goals, it is possible to configure daily deals as a key part of a marketing and sales arsenal.

Turi Altavilla, a seasoned pro mixed martial arts (MMA) league executive—who previously produced massive live Pay Per View (PPV) events for King of the Cage and PRIDE Fight League—began his own amateur promotion, University of MMA (UofMMA.com). Since launch, U of MMA's consistently professional-quality events have become the premier showcase for up-and-coming amateur fighters from around the country and one of the only regular live MMA shows offered in Los Angeles. Though the polished events (frequented by familiar pro MMA faces and Hollywood fight fans) may seem like corporate-funded affairs, they're not; Altavilla and his team operate just like every other small business, intent on sustainable growth.

Try, Try Again

Altavilla considered utilizing a daily deal early after launching the U of MMA, but decided to wait. "Groupon was about huge discounts, and I wasn't comfortable with de-valuing the price of our tickets. If we were only doing one show (and never again), and attendance was terrible, then I'd consider Groupon—because something is better than nothing. But, the issue for us is that we have to come back in two months, and so that model doesn't work for us."

Since expanding to a new venue, however, U of MMA has utilized Living Social to offer a ticket package. "[Living Social] involves a discount, but it's more about a fun activity a couple can do together (which was appealing), and we can also create packages. We add knick-knacks (shirts, baggies, parking) that have value, but that we get for little. So, the customer feels they are getting a good deal and we aren't killing our tickets."

From the outset, Altavilla tread lightly, with an eye on the big picture. "We wanted to be careful not to devalue our brand," he explained. "By the time we moved over to Club Nokia, we already had a strong base of customers and we didn't want to undercut ourselves."

"Our first time using Living Social, we only sold maybe 20 tickets through that platform," Altavilla recalled. "So, if that had been our only experience, it would not have been a big success." But Altavilla expected that, like many other tools, daily deals would require some trial and error.

Tweaking the Package

Another advantage of wading slowly into the daily deal arena was the ability to consider small adjustments to the packages offered. "The first deal, we offered about four different packages," Altavilla said. "I felt the configurations might be a bit too complicated."

The next time U of MMA offered a deal, he tried to simplify the number of packages and added value by offering a free U of MMA T-shirt at the door. "We realized, after the fact, that T-shirts were a little problematic. You can't anticipate what sizes people will want, so it's hard to make sure you have enough of all sizes on hand." They went with a one-size-fits-all U of MMA bag for their next deal.

On their most recent daily deal, which helped garner record-setting attendance at the venue, Altavilla decided to bundle the deal along with discounted venue parking. "What's worked for us overall has been creating a package with added value that can be differentiated from what's sold at the door."

Because floor seats had been selling well, he opted to offer a limited number of upper-level seats only. He noted that vendors have a lot of flexibility on limiting the number of deals they offer and that you can always sell more if you choose later on. "If your deals sell out, they'll ask you if you want to offer more." But Altavilla wisely exercises that option with caution, careful not to flood the market with discounts.

Next Up: Developing Deals for Full-Price Customers

Today, Altavilla is considering how to maintain balance and customer satisfaction for his full-price, regular attendees. He's exploring different ways of offering season tickets or loyalty programs, considering many fight fans connected with the fighters' gyms are familiar repeat customers. "You don't want regulars who pay full price to feel slighted when they see daily deal customers next to them in line," Altavilla said. "No one wants to feel like they overpaid, or someone else got more for the same price."

Again, bundling or offering a completely different set of perks and incentives will be key. "By adding value to whatever packages we're offering, we can differentiate the daily deals from loyalty deals."

By always considering their overall sales and marketing strategy, and anticipating negative blowback that daily deals can cause, Altavilla has been able to make realistic, cost-benefit decisions about how best to utilize those deals and maintain customer satisfaction across all buying segments.

Do: It doesn't matter whether or not you're a designer. Sketch out your ideas on what to present to your audience first on mobile wireframes, either with pen and paper (try bit.ly/UIStencils) or on the iPad (using the AppCooker app).

Don't: Trust that all the content created for your desktop website will translate into a "finger first" format.

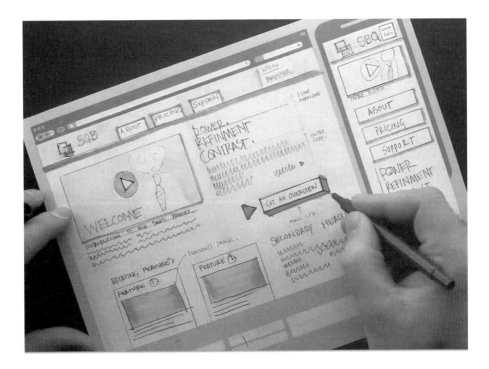

Change Your Future

Riding the Perpetual Whitewater

How can you best prepare for what lies ahead?

We've talked quite a bit about how to implement changes—that is, the proactive, bite-sized steps you can take to change your business and your interactions with customers. But this chapter is a little different.

This chapter is all about looking to the future—*your* future, specifically—and continuing the process of connecting all of the seemingly disparate parts. If only it were as simple as looking into a crystal ball and seeing absolutes that we can anticipate and plan around.

Alas, for all our technology and connectedness, the only constant is change. By continuing to educate and inform yourself about what's happening around you, you can move through the things that affect your life and your business, and start connecting the dots toward fulfillment.

From Perpetual Whitewater to Going With the Ebb and Flow

If you are human and, thus, feeling the constant anxiety that comes with the "perpetual whitewater" of change, it bears repeating that the same technological advances fueling the changes are not quite as stress-producing for the younger set among us. Just understanding that there *is* hope in interacting successfully with the bewildering array of technology, tools, and sheer volume of messages is calming.

Embracing imperfection can lead to much higher satisfaction for your customers, partners, employees, and other stakeholders. Shift away from the fallacy of being an all-knowing expert to someone that can *help others* narrow down choice, based on your expert lens.

The first Tip in this chapter is about being aware of the sources that are relevant to us and putting them into a system that works as our magical daily shot of "keeping up," in whatever time frame we have for that day.

Next, I'll share with you how Brenee Brown's influence has made an immense difference in my business, even from a distance, because I've learned the power of being personally vulnerable. I believe in her statement from *Daring Greatly*: "We are hardwired to connect with others; it's what gives purpose and meaning to our lives, and without it there is suffering."[1] When you understand connection as an innate human need (not want), I hope you will look at our time more as a golden age of connection, than one of overwhelm.

Remember those Ys and Zs we looked at in Tip 45? In Tip 48, I'll proudly introduce you to the Magic Makers that amaze us with their ability to connect young genius to older leaders (who enable those new ideas to make a difference in the world). What can we learn from the way they go about navigating the waters more "lazy-river style" and less "whitewater"?

In Tip 49, I'll teach you how limiting yourself is actually freeing. I give tools that I use every day to limit overwhelm and get it all done.

Finally, we are moving toward a world where giving is a given. To that end, I'll explore how taking up a cause and integrating it into your business checks all the boxes: warm fuzzies *and* a healthier bottom line.

To sign off, I challenge you to think of what you are becoming more efficient for, and to what end. I hope it is (as author and thought leader Seth Godin's musings have taught me so well) to create art from your business acumen and bring it to the world.

Please take a moment, at least, to share your creative journey with me. I look forward to our continued conversation.

Tip 46 Change Yourselfie: How You Custom-Aggregate Useful News

With all of the accessibility that the Internet has afforded, getting your daily dose of news, information, and entertainment can prove to be an overwhelming crush. We seem to have reached an apex of info, where we no longer worry about accessing the media we want. Now, it's a matter of paring it down into the bite-sized morsels that our busy schedules allow.

Take a moment to consider all of the ways in which we now consume information. Then, examine your daily inflow of info in the ways that work best for you. For example, I have bookworm friends who found they just never had time or the attention span to sit down with a book long enough to get into the story. But, by shifting over to podcasts and audible.com downloads on their devices instead, they've been "reading" like crazy, listening to the stories on their work commutes, at the gym, while doing chores, or on the way to and from carpool pickups.

Shifting Media Consumption and Platforms

Through World War II, families crowded around their radios for news updates and episodes of serials like *Little Orphan Annie*. Once TV arrived on the scene, some of that attention shifted to the *Ed Sullivan Show*. Even more hours were spent in front of TVs once color came along, and with the advent of cable channels.

When the Internet became widely available, people spent time surfing websites. Through the years, faster and faster delivery speeds have made live streaming and instant viewing from Netflix and Amazon a daily reality. We've never really given up any of these channels fully. Somehow, like a delectable dessert, there's always room for more.

Now, vast media gorging is a part of daily life, with many receiving most of their info and entertainment via online sources. In fact, recent studies predict daily media consumption at a whopping 15.5 hours per person, per day by 2015,[2] our simultaneous device addictions compounding the time.

No one would think to plop in front of the TV for almost all of their waking hours each and every day, but we think nothing of being online and streaming radio or podcasts throughout our workday and into the evening hours. Some even hang with that TV while Tweeting, texting, and keeping a laptop open, too.

Even seniors have shifted their media consumption significantly in a few short years: According to the Pew Charitable Trusts' information on technology and media usage, about 35 percent of seniors were online in 2008, compared to 59 percent as of 2014.

Your Magical Magazine

Say you're on an outbound plane, or a faraway beach, or anywhere in the world where you can just sit peacefully for one minute and, say, peruse a magazine. This magazine, as it happens, is a magical magazine. It knows exactly what you want to read about and contains content from all of your favorite publications, blogs, and people, all rolled into one simple-to-navigate, constantly updated, completely customized source of reading nirvana. Well, happy days, because that informational utopia exists in the here and now—and if you aren't already, you should tap into that magic.

I happen to use Feedly for this purpose, but have also enjoyed Flipboard. Pocket, which allows you to "clip" video feeds in addition to save websites you want to read later, is another popular choice. The beautiful thing is that you aren't limited to the types of feeds you can source from.

Keep Good Company

In addition to news and entertainment reading selections, tap into your business community and news through your RSS feed selection. For instance, blogs by business leaders within your industry can be one of the best sources of relevant advice, insight, and wisdom for the busy entrepreneur (such as an excellent little blog called ChunkofChange.com, for example)!

Often, small business owners are entrenched in the day-to-day activities of running their businesses and feel like they don't have time to keep tabs on the vast universe of industry data. That's the great thing about seeking out a select few business bloggers that really represent what matters to your business: following their feeds and reading their posts feels like getting the "Best Of" lowdown from a trusted insider.

Keep an open mind about your news sources, as well. I actually get quite a lot of news—real, relevant, immediate information—from Twitter, which isn't just a place where hipsters post about pop culture. When choosing your favorite feeds, look to Twitter, Facebook, and YouTube channels for very specific, targeted info.

Tip 47 Pull Back the Curtain to Connect

We are all frightened of exposing our personal vulnerabilities in many "arenas" (work, personal, with partners, in public) of our lives and, yet, it's likely that our fear is grossly misplaced. Our "fight or flight" reaction to irrational fears is an evolutionary remnant. It's causing our brains to believe that our contribution to a meeting, quick blog video, or exposure by commenting in online communities as our authentic selves, is equivalent to putting our naked bodies in front of a hungry lion. Add a dose of perfectionism, and there have been many times where I've personally felt as though I will never be good enough.

Give Them a Reason to "Like" You!

People do business with people they like. You and your brand can choose to always start the conversation from a place of empathy. True empathy builds trust.

Sympathy, on the other hand, does not. Sympathy belongs in cards that recognize someone's passing, not as a foundation with your customer base.

In a business setting, starting conversations with leads or customers from a place of recognizing the underlying emotion will connect, whereas if you just focus merely on experience, it'll fall flat.

Today, I thrive on the pursuit of excellence (not perfection)—a very inward driver. I'm conscious of the external-facing, people-pleasing parts in me, but am no longer paralyzed by them. If you identify with me, then, right now, give yourself permission to take over the wheel and move fear out of the driver's seat. It'll still be there, riding shotgun, but fear won't control the speed or put on the brakes. Research confirms that it is precisely when we show our vulnerability, when we show our humanity, that we connect with others.

I forced myself to reveal my story in the intro to this book. When writing, it was the part that I left to the bitter end, starting and stopping again, so hungry to get it "just right." Yet, in the end, I just put myself out there.

Brenee Brown reminds us that humans are *hardwired* to connect, and that no one connects substantively with a mask. She defines courage as:

- Asking for what you need.
- Speaking your truth.
- Owning your story.
- Setting boundaries.
- Reaching out for support.

When you realize, as I did, that personal vulnerability is not weakness, but rather an opportunity to connect, it becomes a very powerful force.

Tip 48 Tap Into the Best of Generation Z

As a society, we think fondly of seeing the world "through the eyes of a child." Something about that blend of innocence, simplicity, and pure excitement appeals to us.

But, for some reason, all that changes once those children turn into teens. Now, their perspective is too much, too fast, too loud, too radical. Suddenly, their unique way of seeing life, unfiltered and without conventional limitations, seems unruly and even slightly dangerous.

To look ahead and keep the freshest perspective, we need to reevaluate and embrace the wisdom *we* can learn from the best and the brightest of Generation Z. This up-and-coming crew maintains that innocence and simplicity and injects it straight into their problem-spotting—and problem-*solving*.

I'm not talking about an airy-fairy, feel-good "I believe the children are our future" stuff, but rather, mind-blowing, inspiring business lessons and insight for even the most grizzled entrepreneur. It starts with a willingness to engage, listen, and learn without fear or irrational aversion.

The Kids Are Naturals

I didn't have a cell phone in high school. I only started using e-mail once I went away to college, and it took me some time to understand that I didn't need to write an actual *letter*, but could just drop a line—and even send that line to several people at once!

The newest generation has never lived life unplugged. Ever.

I spoke about the topic of teens with writer Melissa Jun Rowley, who is (among many other hyphens and hats) an award-winning journalist, on-air host, and producer, with a passion for all things tied to the convergence of technology and social innovation. "When I was 15," the 30-something Rowley told me, "I was getting in trouble and was completely self-involved and didn't know what was really going on in the world. And I think that teenagers today...they are able to access information in ways that that other generations have never been able to, and that's because of the Internet. And they're able to collaborate with kids in other parts of the world because of emerging technology. And they're able to just understand things a little bit more in depth I think than when we were teenagers; I mean, they've never known a time without the Internet. Every generation keeps just advancing more and more. And there is so much flack that the Millennial generation is given for being self-entitled and not really knowing what's going on in the world. I don't actually completely agree with that."

Magic Makers

Some of the teens featured by Melissa Jun Rowley on her *Magic Makers* program are truly astounding, such as:

- Jack Andraka (b. 1997), grand prize winner of the 2012 Intel International Science and Engineering Fair for developing a faster, cheaper test to isolate a protein marker indicative of pancreatic, ovarian, and lung cancers.
- Elif Bilgin (b. 1997), developed a bioplastic made from banana peels after two years of trial and error, garnering her the 2013 Scientific American Science in Action prize.

How to Engage

Of her many projects focused on the intersection of tech and social innovation, Rowley created *Magic Makers*, a social impact series that follows a group of teens as they use STEAM (science, technology, engineering, art, and math) to advance humanity. The forward-thinking entrepreneur and activist Rowley views the indefatigability and unencumbered thinking of today's teens as inspiring: "When I talk to the kids...they're just so optimistic and they're so imaginative, and they're positive."

The gifted teens she has featured on *Magic Makers* also intuitively combine their gifts with truly meaningful goals. "What drew me to them really was that they're so entrepreneurial at such young ages—and they're humanitarian about it," Rowley shared. "You know, no one told Jack Andraka that he should use his scientific genius to develop a new method for detecting pancreatic cancer. He did that on his own...because somebody very close to him died from pancreatic cancer. So the fact that he combined his gift with helping others at such an early age—I mean, I think he was 15 when he developed this idea."

Though the genius of these extraordinary teens cannot be denied, Rowley thinks there's a cultural evolution occurring, as well: "The projects, and the real brilliance that we're seeing coming out of this generation.... It's partly that the kids I selected for the show...they're all tremendously motivated and gifted. But it's also just a sign of the times."

Fluid Access

"Back in the day," as the saying goes, a respectable individual had to have a formal letter of introduction from a direct friend or acquaintance in order to approach a stranger. Until recently, in fact, an individual had to work his or her way into an organization, and through bureaucratic gatekeepers, to gain access to the top decision-makers, thinkers, and innovators.

Today, with the interconnectedness that the Internet affords, anyone can quickly become a part of a niche community, and tap into the upper echelons of management and creativity with a quick comment, e-mail, or direct message.

This open communication doesn't necessarily derive from audacity. Kids just don't know they *can't* or *shouldn't* communicate openly. They simply see someone of stature as being cool and in-the-know—and safely accessible through the detached medium of Internet communication. Worst-case scenario, they get no response. No biggie.

But, more often than not nowadays, academic and industry leaders respond, impressed by the level of interest and enthusiasm only a young person can channel, and the directness of communication (what used to be called "moxie").

So, how can you, too, engage with bright, forward-thinking teens?

First, make yourself open to incoming inquiries. Then, seek out interactive, creative forums to observe, listen, and engage with smart young people. There are so many ways to accomplish this, such as:

- Finding online communities (through Facebook, Instagram, and Reddit, to name a few).

- Exploring talks, programs, and fairs offered by local colleges (particularly high-level math and science institutions or creative havens, where art and technology are bound to intersect).

- Through mentoring programs, aimed at high-achieving students (such as mock trial organizations, advanced creative exhibitions, invention, and innovation contests).

- Participating in local civic events aimed at effectuating social change.

- Checking out videos, podcasts, or other media highlighting the ideas and accomplishments of young innovators (like Melissa Jun Rowley's *Magic Makers*).

However you choose to tap into the younger generation, just do so with an open mind. There's a lot you can learn about how teens think, as well as how you should approach them as a target market and train them to focus their talents as employees and collaborators.

Tip 49 How to Do It All Going Forward

You must understand that, in order to optimize your business, website, and (well) life, means that you are always coming from a place of limited resources (because we are all human), but also unlimited possibility (because we are all human).

Limit Yourself, By Choice

In the ultimate paradox, it turns out that our plethora of choices, which we equate with freedom and happiness, is anything but. Psychologist Barry Schwartz's look at societies with great abundance found "where individuals are offered more freedom and choice (personal, professional, material) than ever before—are now witnessing near-epidemic levels of depression."[3]

In his thought-provoking TED Talk, Schwartz mused, "We can go to watch our kid play soccer, and we have our [devices]...even if they're all shut off, every minute that we're watching our kid mutilate a soccer game, we are also asking ourselves, 'Should I answer this cell phone call? Should I respond to this e-mail? Should I draft this letter?' And even if the answer to the question is 'no,' it's certainly going to make the experience of your kid's soccer game very different than it would've been. So everywhere we look, big things and small things, material things and lifestyle things, life is a matter of choice. [In the past] not everything was a matter of choice. And the question is, is this good news, or bad news? And the answer is yes."

Many times, the more choices that are available lead to the complete paralysis of indecision. Schwartz cites one study where the sheer number of Vanguard mutual fund choices in a company's 401k correlated to reduced participation. Specifically, participation rate went down by 2 percent for every 10 additional mutual funds offered. Why? He states, "It's so damn hard to decide that you'll put it off until tomorrow...and then tomorrow never comes."

Psychologist Sheena Iyengar is famous for an experiment in a luxury food store, whereby researchers set up a sampling of jams. Sometimes there were six choices, other times 24. Shoppers flocked to the table with more samples, but were more likely to purchase if they were presented with less. Those who chose from the smaller number were 10 times more likely to be buyers, proving that more is less. As discussed in a *New York Times* article that references her work, "More choice is not always better, she suggests, but neither is less. The optimal amount of choice lies somewhere in between infinity and very little, and that optimum depends on context and culture. 'In practice, people can cope with larger assortments than research on our basic cognitive limitations might suggest,' Iyengar writes. 'After all, visiting the cereal aisle doesn't usually give shoppers a nervous breakdown.'"[4]

Go With the Flow

By first developing an awareness of how much of your day is spent looking at choices, you may be able to develop a system that ultimately gives you more satisfaction while getting stuff done, too. What works for me is to constantly prioritize and optimize (small change adds up!) within the understanding that there will always be three limited resources to balance:

1. Time.
2. Money.
3. Information.

Understand that to maximize is a myth. You cannot maximize your time; you can only *optimize* it. You cannot truly multitask, but you can do several things at once if you understand that only one of those things will get done well, and none excellent.

Even if you had all the money in the world to throw at a problem, you may not have the right information to solve it. It is liberating, weirdly, to discover the boundaries we all operate in.

How to Do It All?

First, and most importantly, you need what I call the "breathing room" to take a moment to see it all from a 20,000-foot view. Very few people I know have this discipline.

Promise yourself that, in that moment, for 15 minutes in the morning, while enjoying a vista and your cup of joe, or a physical re-boot through exercise, you will live fully and let all other concerns just move through you. Some people meditate, and I commend those people. I haven't found that sweet spot; it's not a strength of mine.

What I've found is, allowing my brain to have the deep breath in order to make the connections that naturally form with room; it gives me perspective. Then, prioritizing (limiting choice to what is important) becomes second-nature and the constant change of today's demands are no longer stressful.

This is actually a creative exercise and it takes practice. It's art, disguised as work—and, many times, messy. It may not work the first, or even seventh, time, but make it a habit to give yourself the gift of breathing room every day and everything slowly comes into focus. Then, once your etch-a-sketch scatter brain has been gently reset, sit back down and take a deep dive back into the stuff with your priority machete.

Carry It Through to Your Business

Give your consumers the gift of relieving them from the burden of all these unhappy-making decisions by curating things for them, but balance it with the reality that we all still like having choices. Be okay with the messy "art" of that balance.

As a retailer, you might create groupings of top products with a review note giving a quick reassurance of why they made the right choice. An excellent example of this is the wine aisle at my local Trader Joe's, where I see the employee favorites, graphic cards stating the quick flavor notes and characteristics and limited time batches that I wouldn't want to miss.

This is done online by categories, top lists, and featured products and articles. This also applies to the choices on a website's menu, pull-down, how many social sharing buttons to have, etc. In e-mail, try to stick with one offer. Smart salespeople know that when it comes time to close the sale, three choices will do better than 30.

Tip 50 Embrace Community Giving

I have written about community giving numerous times on ChunkofChange.com, primarily because I believe that you can gain so much—that intangible, really deep-down kind of benefit—from incorporating some form of giving back into your work and personal life.

This Tip revolves around bringing those actions into your business life in a meaningful way, purposefully cross-pollinating these two areas so that you can magnify your positive efforts. The idea is twofold: bring awareness and additional support to your organization by promoting its goals to your clientele, and garner additional respect and possibly bring in work from the organization's existing base of supporters.

Overall impact: a sudden and organic boost to your own efforts.

Choose One Cause to Focus On

Even the coldest-hearted Grinch or busiest multitasker cares about *something*. And that's a good place to start. There are thousands upon thousands of nonprofit organizations that you might support.

Find a group you can personally invest in, something that aligns with your core values. There are so many hyper-specific organizations that there must be one that speaks to your heart.

Wear Your Heart on Your Sleeve

In order to incorporate your community giving into your business, you have to communicate about it with your clients somehow. So put your thinking cap on, and maybe have your employees participate in this brainstorm to figure out new and resourceful ways to blend your corporate giving and *partnering* with other organizations that have similar initiatives.

It takes a lot to get someone's real attention in this whirring world we now live in. An effective mashup campaign likely entails more than simply telling clients about your support. So, approach your campaign to communicate your organizational support just as you would apply your marketing acumen and creativity elsewhere in your business. Catch the eye; make the connection memorable. Remember: a little razzmatazz never hurt no one.

For example, I did a Chunk of Change write-up[5] on a notable effort put in play by the beachy Pacific Edge Hotel, which placed an adorable stuffed animal embroidered with the name of its nonprofit partner, Pacific Marine Mammal Center, on every room's bed. Purchasing the stuffed animal gave guests a lovely reminder of their stay that also happened to benefit the Center's mission of helping SoCal coastal mammals. Cue the good customer feelings all around—but for all the right reasons.

In my own business, ohso! design, I also decided to take another tack to engage my clients regarding our spotlight organization: Standup for the Cure. Instead of just including a little note at the bottom of invoices mentioning our support, I incorporated a new policy to share some ownership and pride of involvement with my clients. Instead of donating "a portion of the proceeds from their account," we now tie our donated time *directly* to the client's paid invoices.

Engage in That Community

There is also so much to gain on the other side of the equation, the organization's side. By partnering with a particular group, you are tapping into a preexisting community of likeminded individuals. By actively and sincerely participating in the group's activities and outreach, you are opening up a doorway to a whole new group of potential customers and/or referrers.

As we've talked about throughout this book, in a world of endless choice, people are always looking for ways to differentiate one option from the next. Sharing a common cause/organization adds to your UVP in the best way, giving others within that community yet another reason to choose you over other people.

> **Be Totally Lazy—Still Give Back**
>
> No matter how busy you are, giving back is so easy nowadays, you can literally do *nothing* and still make a difference. So seriously, no excuses.
>
> Through programs like AmazonSmile and PayForward (PayForward.com), you simply designate who you want to donate to when you shop. AmazonSmile (a retailer) gives a percentage of the sale, whereas PayForward donates an instant refund. All you have to do is shop as you normally would.

What the Research Says With Dr. Norah Dunbar

As a professor of communication and a researcher who studies the communication processes of interpersonal relationships, people often ask me what I think about the effects of new technologies on how we communicate with one another. If you go to a restaurant, you see people sitting at a table, and rather than talking to one another, they are looking at their devices. If you go to a movie, people have their phones out despite the "no texting" warnings ahead of the feature. If you go to the park, parents are sitting on benches with their phones out instead of playing with their children.

Is this the destruction of interpersonal communication? Or is it a re-invention of it? I spend my life surrounded by "digital natives" who are so used to technology that they integrate new forms easily into their everyday life. They post reviews about the restaurant while they are eating at it. They tweet about a movie while they are in it. They take pictures of their kids and post them on Facebook while they are still at the park. Digital natives keep many relationships going at once and interact with multiple people on a variety of topics simultaneously.

This book has provided excellent examples of this very phenomenon from a business perspective, as the various chapters consider different aspects of marketing, and the final chapter urges you to consider all these parts as an integrated whole. Just as people have integrated technology into every facet of their lives, businesses need to think about how they fit into that new way of thinking. If people can order their groceries on an app while they wait for a train, or chat with a friend in China while eating lunch alone in L.A., how can your business take advantage of these snippets of time to interact with customers? In my opinion, the close relationships formed over three martini lunches à la *Mad Men* are gone. Instead, you might only get a few moments to make an impression and win over a customer. They might see your ad on their phone, or come across your website in their Google search results, or scan your QR code in the grocery store but you need to be ready to jump on the opportunity while you have it.

I don't think interpersonal relationships, in life or in business, are dead, but they certainly have changed. Keep up and enjoy the ride.

In the Real World: John Lee Dumas Is Putting It All Together

I really struggled with where to include Entrepreneur on Fire master-mind John Lee Dumas in this book. With this gentleman, it's really a quality problem; he's doing things right in so many ways, it's difficult to decide on just one thing to highlight.

I decided that the final "In the Real World" section of the final chapter would be ideal. That's because perhaps the most impressive aspect of Dumas is not necessarily all of his successful actions, but his overall approach to his work, e-commerce, connecting with his audience, and continuing a constant cycle of learning and improvement.

One of the truly notable aspects of Dumas's operation comes from his complete business transparency with his audience. I mean, the guy literally posts his monthly profit and loss reports—and discusses those P&Ls in scheduled podcasts (some of his top-rated shows, I might add). Although not all of us might be comfortable with opening our books for all the world to see, it's just one way that Dumas has differentiated himself within the business marketplace—and garnered a strong affinity with his listener-base.

Ever-Evolving UVP

Given Dumas's raging success, one of my first questions for him focused on his UVP. Someone so successful must have a rock-solid, immoveable UVP, right? "So, this is a great question, Olga," he told me, "because it's one where, even where I'm sitting at today with EOF, I'm still struggling with on some levels. Because it is doing just that: It's evolving. And as different external forces come into play, and the business grows to different sizes and levels and reach, we need to continue to adapt and to adjust, even if we want to keep going on that same course."

Then, he provided a great analogy: "It's almost like you take off from San Diego on a plane ride to New York City, you start heading on a bearing...but you need to adjust that bearing a million times between your destinations because of the wind, the wind pressure that changes, the speed... any external forces that may actually knock you just a little bit off course, to continue, you always have to be adjusting that."

Advice From an Avatar

How does that adjustment process proceed?

"For me, it always does come back to the avatar," Dumas explained. For Entrepreneur on Fire, Dumas has developed "Jimmy," his rendering of his ideal podcast listener. An avatar is an icon or figure representing a particular person. In business application, an avatar is a representation of your ideal client/customer. A business may have multiple avatars representing several target demographics. (Review Chapter 1's Do This Not That for help in developing your own avatar or even group of personas.)

MEET JIMMY

"That's where I really like to look at my unique selling proposition and ask, 'Who is that one perfect listener for me that I truly need to keep as my North Star?'.... That helps me focus in on that perfect listener for EOF, so I can ensure that I'm always serving that one perfect listener that I created that podcast for in the first place."

Whenever he and his team feel unsure of what direction to take, he simply asks, "WWJD? What would Jimmy do?" By considering the question through "Jimmy's" eyes, instead of his own, Dumas feels confident and clear about his UVP course corrections.

He also taps into Jimmy's mind through a constant feedback loop with his listeners and customers. "It's really by the daily e-mails, Tweets, social media messages that we get from a thankful audience. I read those, I respond to those, I listen to those. I'm always engaging and asking my audience for feedback and for what they're struggling with so I can continue to keep my finger on their pulse. Because that's so important, to really know if my audience is changing, if what I'm doing is becoming...is starting to fall on deaf ears or needs to be spiced up a little bit, or if the format we currently have is still resonating with them. So that's a huge focus of ours that we continue to look at on a day-to-day basis."

Systematic Approach

A critical component to Dumas's success has been building internal systems that allow him to delegate tasks to his team to free him up to build the business. I asked where he had learned how to do this so effectively. Dumas cites Parkinson's Law as just one valuable concept instilled in him from his time in the Army: *Tasks will expand to the time you allot them.*

"The overriding mentality that I have, Olga, is one of abundance. I am a believer of having the abundance mentality and putting out as much free, valuable, consistent content to the world, and let the chips fall where they may. I really avoid the scarcity mindset of really thinking that if I take a bigger piece of the pie, that someone else is getting a smaller piece, and vice versa."

—John Lee Dumas, Entrepreneuronfire.com

"I really do have to point to, at 22 years old, being commissioned as an officer in the U.S. Army," he said. "And then spending the next four years as a second and first lieutenant, and then a captain... and having growing responsibilities throughout those four years." He cited the top-down management, military discipline, structure, and focus as making a major impression on him as a future businessman. "It really awed me, I was inspired by it, and I took a lot of those lessons and skills that I learned as an officer and applied them to the entrepreneurial world, and they definitely have worked out well."

DO this not that

Do: Change up your working environment and use systems as a way of making time to connect, brainstorm, get creative, and innovate!

Don't: Fall into the mentality that systems are tools that solely maximize production.

Because this book aims to give little insights on how to build a better mousetrap, in terms of your business efforts, I spent a lot of time talking about ways to optimize limited resources and increase efficiency. Systems are critical to efficient production and providing a consistent customer experience, no doubt. But to what end?

Remember: the best thing about that "better mousetrap" is that it gives the cat time to play, think, and brainstorm on his company's next vermin-catching contraption.

Don't Use Systems to Build a House of Cards

When it comes to creative endeavors and small businesses that rest on the tireless shoulders of a mighty few, systems serve a far more important purpose than simply cranking out more, more, more. In fact, truth be told, if you fall into this fallacious mindset, you will end up mighty disappointed—because production and creativity will actually decline. As much as we want to be on 24/7, readily available by device at all times, that's a formula with diminishing returns.

Consider sleep, for example: Every animal *needs* sleep to recharge the brain, organize the day's massive influx of data, and regulate the nervous system. How do we know this? Because lack of sleep contributes to the development of serious health problems, such as depression, mental fog, impaired motor skills, and more. Likewise, looking at your efficiency efforts as a way of piling more and more onto your company's to-do lists will only end up in an ugly crash and burn. What systems *can* provide people is extra time and much needed mental space.

Forward-Thinking Corporate Collectives

Though it isn't generally open to the public, some lucky outsiders (like my friend, SMB attorney and mom Caroline Rath) have been able to tour the Nickelodeon Animation Studios in Burbank, California. And, from the sound of it, the powers that be really took it seriously to incorporate all of the fun, silliness, and creativity the kids' TV channel is known for into their main animation hub.

"When I visited with my daughter's class several years ago," Caroline told me, "I enjoyed seeing how Nickelodeon created an open, creative space where their animation staff could playfully interact, all while working together in a very organized, systematic way to meet their production deadlines."

This included a centralized, open kitchen/dining area where employees could congregate, as well as a basketball court for downtime or even working one-on-one sessions. Even the cubicles and walls, the bane of office workers across America, served an interactive purpose: they were made out of dry erase board surfaces that could be doodled on by their occupants— or passing coworkers.

"I liked that the overall vibe at the Nickelodeon Animation Studio didn't seem geared solely toward faster production for higher output," Caroline says. "Not at all. It seemed clear, even as a casual observer, that the production structure—the creative assembly line—was a priority to all the employees we met. But the emphasis on interaction and a strong element of play showed that team-building and the fostering of creativity were equally as important, for both employee job satisfaction and also to the quality of the shows they produced."

Corporate "Campus" Life

Some of these changes in how large corporations operate can be gleaned from the change in their internal nomenclature. For example, tech behemoth Google, which prides itself on doing pretty much everything outside of the box, doesn't call its massive 26-acre hub in Mountain View, California, something conventional like "corporate headquarters." Au contraire! They call it the Googleplex campus.

Similarly, the Dreamworks Animation Studios also calls its Glendale home a "campus." And this comports with the similar aims of both companies to keep their employees creative, inspired, and committed to continual learning—all with the end goal of stoking innovation.

Toward that end, the Dreamworks Animation campus is modeled after a luxe Mediterranean setting, complete with a picturesque lagoon where employees can lunch, lounge, and (literally) draw inspiration. Like Google, Dreamworks also provides its talent with free food—because no one can think, let alone get creative, without proper body and mind fuel.

Google Job Perks

Google views the mental energy and creativity of its Googlers as its most valuable asset. Thus, the company makes sure that Googleplex employees have ample rest and relaxation, food (and caffeine!), and creative and inspirational outlets available on-site, such as:

- On-campus restaurants that serve free meals to employees throughout the day.
- Free campus bikes to scoot from here to there.
- Free massages for employees.

- Volleyball court, tennis court, baseball field, and multiple fitness centers.
- Nap pods for some quick shut-eye or quiet thinking.
- Random art-related stuff (giant dinosaur skeleton with flamingos inside; scads of public art; a statue garden).
- Two organic gardens. (Where do you think the restaurants get their produce?)
- Solar-powered electric car charging station.

Personal Application

Downtime is not "lazy" or "unproductive"; it's necessary for sanity and creativity, which every entrepreneur has to exhibit in his or her problem-solving, no matter how technical the enterprise. Make sure to take regular vacations, spending days—no, weeks!—away from the office, nurturing your creative soul and sipping umbrella drinks beachside, while enjoying twice-daily massages.

Of course, I'm kidding; we aren't living in Denmark's government-sponsored paid time off system! But give your brain a break here and there, and encourage interaction and team problem-solving among your team members instead of cramming in more and more working lunch meetings. Working a little less can indeed result in working more productively. We all need your innovation to push us forward.

Notes

Introduction

1. *http://online.wsj.com/news/articles/SB10001424052702304 55880457937678191532752 4?KEYWORDS=subway&mg= reno64-wsj&url=http%3A%2F%2Fonline.wsj.com%2Farti cle%2FSB1000142405270230455880457937 6781915327524. html%3FKEYWORDS%3Dsubway*

Chapter 1

1. *www.myfoxla.com/story/24805921/the-grilled-cheese-truck*
2. *http://ideamensch.com/dave-danhi/*
3. *http://articles.latimes.com/2011/may/06/food/ la-fo-food-trucks-20110506*
4. *www.sba.gov/content/marketing-101-basics*
5. *http://nccs.urban.org/statistics/quickfacts.cfm.*
6. *www.businesswire.com/news/home/20121004005444/en/ Standup-Cure-Awarded-Top-Philanthropic-Effort-Honors#. U0hb7tybmAM.*
7. *www.zaneschweitzer.com/ZanesWorld/Home.html*

Chapter 2

1. Altimeter's original Crowdspring assign-ment page: *www.crowdspring.com/logo-design/*

project/374189_logo-for-social-mediaweb-20-thought-leader-charlene-li/

2. Altimeter Blog post from 2009: www.altimetergroup.com/2009/06/redesign-and-logo-for-altimeter-group.html

Chapter 3

1. www.nydailynews.com/life-style/one-third-u-s-marriages-start-online-dating-study-article-1.1362743

2. www.zendesk.com/resources/customer-service-and-lifetime-customer-value

3. http://onlinelibrary.wiley.com/doi/10.1111/j.1083-6101.2010.01528.x/full

4. https://sites.google.com/site/webmasterhelpforum/en/faq--crawling--indexing---ranking

5. www.awa-digital.com/blog/case-study/cro-case-study-northern-parrots-homepage/%23.U_fepUtoKAM

Chapter 4

1. www.quora.com/Web-Analytics/Should-conversion-rate-be-measured-against-visits-or-unique-visitors

Chapter 5

1. www.chunkofchange.com/2013/07/seth-godin-inspiration/

2. http://sherpablog.marketingsherpa.com/email-marketing/email-deliverability-how-a-marketing-vendor-treats-single-opt-in-vs-double-opt-in/

3. www.buzzfeed.com/mylestanzer/boomshakalaka-stanford-bros-create-short-shorts-for-frat-sta%23jg2nvw

4. http://newmediaandnonprofits.org/articles_by_author/17/63/

Chapter 6

1. www.internetretailer.com/2013/12/30/one-ecommerce-platform-rule-them-all

2. http://en.wikibooks.org/wiki/Intellectual_Property_and_the_Internet/Electronic_commerce

3. *www.internetretailer.com/2014/05/13/ digital-marketing-firm-declares-paid-search-dead*

4. *http://it.toolbox.com/blogs/insidecrm/redefining-crm-in-todays- connected-world-an-interview-with-forrester-research-analyst- kate-leggett-60984*

Chapter 7

1. *www.chunkofchange.com/2013/06/ business-owners-hate-yelp-and-business-owners*

2. *www.yelp-press.com/phoenix.zhtml?c=250809&p=irol-press*

3. *www.emarketer.com/Article/ Moms-Place-Trust-Other-Consumers/1007509*

Chapter 8

1. *www.briansolis.com/2014/05/ connected-customers-invisible-value-demographics/.*

Chapter 9

1. *http://searchengineland. com/10-local-marketing-myths-hamstringing-biz-184898*

2. *www.internetretailer.com/commentary/2014/05/20/ what-will-it-take-get-small-business-mobile-commerce.*

3. *http://lbpost.com/life/2000003255-orn-hansen-brings-ameri- can-made-goods-to-the-corner#.U5VocJSwLx4.*

Chapter 10

1. *www.amazon.com/Daring-Greatly- Courage-Vulnerable-Transforms/ dp/1592407331*

2. *http://ucsdnews.ucsd.edu/pressrelease/u.s._media_consump- tion_to_rise_to_15.5_hours_a_day_per_person_by_2015.*

3. *www.ted.com/speakers/barry_schwartz*

4. *www.nytimes.com/2010/04/18/books/review/Postrel-t. html?pagewanted=all&_r=0.*

5. *www.chunkofchange.com/2014/01/giving-back/.*

Index

About the Author

At the ripe age of 24, **Olga Mizrahi** started her career where most finish: as an instructor for the University of California, Irvine extension, where she served as one of the first Web design instructors in Southern California. In the then-untamed wilderness of the late-1990s Internet, she soon found her technical skills in high demand in the private sector, where a former student convinced her to work in-house for financial giant PIMCO. Mizrahi eventually spearheaded several successful Web ventures as director of e-commerce in industries ranging from apparel to vitamins. After securing her MBA from Pepperdine University, Mizrahi launched her own local boutique creative agency, ohso! design, as a vehicle to deliver design-minded marketing services executed with top-notch technical know-how.

Mizrahi finds it extremely rewarding to help small businesses develop their marketing and branding vision, and then put that vision into action. She has also had the opportunity to observe the universality of many of the struggles her clients—from Dole to the local pediatric clinic. To address these challenges, she created easy-to-follow tips and systems that any business owner can implement.

Mizrahi created her blog, ChunkofChange.com, as an extension of the tools she developed to assist her clients better define their Unique Value Proposition (UVP) and effectively carry that message through to results. In doing so, she has come full circle, returning to her teaching roots, distilling information down into manageable (but meaningful) how-to tips that empower small business owners to make small changes that can nonetheless have a significant impact on their bottom line. That practical advice has extended to her local business column in the *Long Beach Post*.

Olga Mizrahi resides in Long Beach, California, with her husband and elementary-aged daughter. She enjoys serving on various advisory boards, which have included the Interactive Advisory board for PBS SoCal, LinkedOC, the California Women's Conference, and the Women's Business Council of the Long Beach Chamber of Commerce.

Let's Continue the Conversation

- linkedin.com/in/olgamizrahi
- @olgamizrahi
- fb.com/chunkofchange
- @chunkofchange
- chunkofchange.com